ON LOVE AND TRAVEL

A MEMOIR

ERIN ZELINKA

WHOLE NARANJA PRESS

"...she was becoming herself and daily casting aside that fictitious self which we assume like a garment with which to appear before the world."

— KATE CHOPIN, *THE AWAKENING*

On Love and Travel
Copyright © 2023 by Erin Zelinka

Cover Design by Tyler Johnson
Photo by Ariel Foletto from Pexels
Spanish Review by Tachi Alvarino Mass

ISBN-13: 979-8-9868885-1-4 (ebook)
ISBN-13: 979-8-9868885-0-7 (paperback)

Follow online for photos and news!
@onloveandtravel
www.onloveandtravel.com

For Mya

May you always be so free
from what other people think.

YOUR HEAD'S GONNA KILL YOU

"I can see your aura," the old man said. "Purple."

Here we go, I thought. Yet another scammer trying to make money off the *gringa* who already paid hundreds of dollars for the guided hike to Machu Picchu. But, being a little desperate, thinking maybe my aura was special and this crackpot held the key to my corroded happiness, I turned around and sat back down at the desk of the Cusco tour agency in the back of a cluttered souvenir shop. Elías, my post-divorce Peruvian lover, sat down at my side.

The man, called Ibán, looked at the blue knit bracelet Elías had made for me, on my left wrist.

"You should wear purple on your left side," he said. "It will help your heart and your head."

"Okay," I said, wondering what purple bracelet he might try to sell me after this little reading.

"Hold out your hands," Ibán said. "Like this."

I did as he demonstrated, extending both arms straight out in front of me with clenched fists facing downward. He extended his arms beneath my own, with his palms facing upward.

"Open your hands," he said. Though our palms were eight inches apart from one another's, it felt burning hot. It was much more than the standard warmth that you would feel emanating from any warm-blooded being.

"Do you feel that?" he asked.

"Yes," I said, still skeptical but unable to deny the sensation.

He continued in English with a thick accent. "You have a very old soul. Some two hundred eighty years. Your heart is antique, but your mind is new." He tilted his chin down and peered over his wire-rimmed old-lady glasses to make eye contact, and he said, slowly, "If you don't stop your head, your head's gonna kill you someday." He held the stare to ensure that I understood. I nodded.

"Do you have a river where you live?" he asked.

"Yes, in my hometown there's a very famous river."

"Go there, to a spot you enjoy, and find a black stone. A small one you can hold in your hand. Tell the stone what you have in your head, your heart, your stomach." He paused. "You have too much ideas, too much feelings, and a lot of anger in your stomach."

I wasn't an angry person. This guy had me all wrong. I had never yelled at anyone or even expressed anger. I looked over at Elías, who held a stoic expression, and I wondered if he agreed.

Ibán continued. "After you tell the stone all, say three times, 'Odín,' the god of the ocean. Afterward you will be really sad. Later, go back to that place where you put the stone. Sit until it's familiar. And you'll feel happy." I nodded, and he continued.

"Someone is going to try to use you in the near future."
Again, the fatherly head tilt. I mentally ran through my life's
current cast of characters, and I couldn't imagine any of
them hurting or using me.

"You are very lucky," he said.

"It's true. I am." Finally something accurate, vague
though it may be. He again made that serious eye contact
and told me one final thing.

"If you can work not just with your head, but with your
heart, you will be very rich."

I waited for him to tell me what the reading would cost
me, certain he had ended on the rich bit to inspire generos-
ity, but Ibán the shaman-salesman never asked for any
money.

HOLY SPIRIT ANIMAL

J ohn proposed a few months after I turned eighteen, when I was still in my senior year of high school with braces and over-plucked eyebrows.

"Will you marry me?" he asked, holding the ring box upside-down as he knelt beside the romantically lit fountain at Lithia Park in Ashland, Oregon.

I bent down to hug him and looked over his shoulder into the treed darkness beyond. I felt no emotion, no excitement, no certainty. So, I did what you do when you don't feel: I analyzed.

I ran a fast mental assessment of the pros and cons. He was good. He was kind. I enjoyed his company. And I heard these words in my head: *No one else will ever love you this much.*

Even more compelling than all that, John was so certain in everything. A product of homeschooling and a fundamentalist Christian upbringing, he knew what we were supposed to believe. I felt certain in nothing, having been brought up by open-minded, free-range parents who had just finalized their long-overdue divorce. I craved the direction that came from John's convictions. I craved his family's homemade apple pies and values and well-worn life path that, it seemed, led to a pretty good life. So I said yes. He could tell me what to think, how to act, who to be. Figuring it all out alone felt too overwhelming.

————

Eight years after John and I married, I laid on my side in bed and cried, hoping he wouldn't hear. Or maybe I did want him to hear. I was capable of crying in silence, but sometimes I'd let whimpers escape. We'd had this talk many times before.

"I'm so unhappy here. I want to go back to the orphanage," I would tell him, referring to the boys' home in Cusco, Peru, where I volunteer-taught English after college graduation. Teaching those scrappy kids, playing soccer together and sipping simple soups, I felt more at home and like myself than ever before or in the five years since.

"I think you need to find your happiness somewhere else, in God."

This only made me cry harder. God. What was God? I didn't feel God, no matter how many Christian books I read or how many Sundays I stood in church, asking Jesus into my heart, waiting for the Holy Spirit to descend on my despair. And I had tried, believe me I had tried. I had read the Bible forwards and backwards. I had read archaeological texts, apologist works and Christian literature. I had watched explanatory documentaries and gone on evangelist missions.

"What is it that you want?" John asked, hoping I'd answer differently this time.

"I want to go to Peru. I want to spend six months there and six months here." This was my idea of compromise. I hated our rural Oregon hometown, the very symbol of suffering in my eyes, and yet, here we were, living here now for three years, building a house three miles from our childhood homes.

"We can't do that. We can't just leave our jobs. We have good jobs."

"We'll get other jobs."

"It's not that easy."

I was always dreaming of big adventures and John was always telling me those dreams weren't prudent. Why was it that everything I wanted was imprudent where his desires were rational?

So, I cried. I prayed that God would make me happy here, with what I had, with who I was. I have a good life, I thought. I should be happy, I thought. I cried harder. If God could hear how much I struggled, maybe He would help me.

I sat up in bed gasping, like the defibrillated dead brought back to life. My phone blinked its rapid red light and cawed the loudest, screaming ring I could find. I answered.

"This is Natalie in dispatch. We've had a homicide and the sheriff wants you to respond."

I rubbed my hand across my face. "I'll be there in an hour."

As the Public Information Officer for a rural sheriff's office, I always had to pick up the phone, twenty-four hours a day, seven days a week. It was an election year, and the sheriff had tasked twenty-seven-year-old me with making the office look good so the tax levy might pass for once.

"What happened? Where are you going?" John asked, as I rolled out of bed and pulled on my thick uniform jacket.

"Homicide. I have to go."

"Is there anything I can help you with?" he said, lying back down.

"No, I just have to get over there." I pulled my stick-straight hair into a ponytail and did a quick makeup job, some blush on my olive skin and a bit of eyeliner, for the cameras.

"Don't drive too fast. He's already dead."

I smiled and gave him a kiss on the cheek. "I won't. Don't worry."

I did, of course, drive fast. Though the victim was dead, the reporters were alive and excited to cross the caution tape for some real news in our county. I arrived exactly one hour from my first communication with dispatch, and I did what I do: I told reporters next to nothing as they shone bright lights in my face on a dark country road.

"The investigation is ongoing...At this time, we are unable to release any further information...The suspect is in custody...There is no threat to the general public...We'll be posting more information as it becomes available."

I tap-danced, I spun, and I twirled around the truth, and they hated me. I couldn't blame them. I hated me, too.

I walked up the gravel driveway in the dark, hearing only the crunch of my boots, with thick woods flanking me on either side. I wasn't armed, and I wished I were, because you never knew who might be running about at a crime scene. When I got to the top, I stared down at the overweight, limp body of a middle-aged woman. I felt nothing.

"What are you doing here?" the detective barked. He and the other detectives had once liked me and even invited me to coffee regularly when I held more secretarial positions, as a records clerk and then a crime analyst. I would jump to assist them with their reports or looking up warrants. But now, with this new position, some treated me as their adversary, locking me out of meetings and withholding whatever they could.

I took a deep breath, preparing for yet another head-butting session. "The sheriff told me to come up here and get the initial report from you."

He scrunched his round head back into his thick neck and scoffed at me. "Well I don't have anything to give you yet, Erin. We're very busy."

"I understand that. I'm just following the sheriff's orders."

"I'll get you information when I can, but we're very busy." He walked over to two other detectives loitering beside a vehicle and took a drink of coffee, laughed and indiscreetly nodded in my direction.

I walked back down the driveway, to the road where more reporters waited with their bright lights and questions about things I couldn't tell them. My heart thumped hard inside my chest, but not because I was afraid of the cameras or the crime scene. No matter what I did—no matter how many courses I took or systems I built or people I helped—I could never win. I had to get out.

When I went for my job interview at the marketing agency, I resented them all, sitting around pub tables, so happy and carefree. Don't you know this is serious, that there is work to be done and worries to be had? I sat on the couch in the lobby in my pencil skirt, legs crossed and a notepad on my lap. The rock music was too loud to think. I needed to think. What year was the company founded? What is its mission? What social media outlets are they currently using? What were my ideas for improvement? Are they playing pool over there? Is that a salad bar?

As part of the application process, the company had asked me to complete a personality test the week prior, but I struggled to fill it out. It was hard to discern which answers were best, what they wanted me to say. I was good at tests, so why was this so difficult? I asked John for help, and he hovered over my shoulder advising on how I felt about things. "No, you don't really care about the aesthetic of a place. Yeah, you value logic over emotion. You value order over creativity."

As I sat in the company foyer, studying my interview notes, a middle-aged man with a five o'clock shadow approached and sat on the armchair adjacent to me. He wore a flat-billed cap, slightly off-center, and leaned forward, clasping his hands. "What's up, chica? I'm Adam. Let's rap."

Chica? Rap? My face was too expressive. I tried to control it so it wouldn't betray my what-a-fucking-idiot reaction. I smiled and sat up straighter, answering his questions but considering walking out the door.

We stepped into an office with bean bags on the floor and motivational posters on the wall. A handsome, tanned man with salt-and-pepper hair sat on the desk, and a pretty woman named Diane leaned back on a leather couch with her arms crossed. I sat on the couch next to her, and Adam sat on a high stool opposite me. He clasped his hands together and started to fire off questions.

"Do you like salad? What kind of music do you like? What's your spirit animal?"

I kept looking down at my typed, bulleted list of memorized answers about strengths and weaknesses, recommendations, qualifications, GPA (a 4.12, thank you very much, please bring that up). They didn't seem to care about any of that.

"Uh-oh, country music, that could be a deal breaker," Adam said, grinning.

"You have an awesome smile!" said the man on the desk, named Jim. Diane giggled.

The door swung open and a young blonde guy in a tank top came bouncing in and wrapped his arms around Jim. He pinched his nipples.

"Aghhhh, Jimbo, you handsome son-of-a-bitch, I can't even take it!" My eyes must have been wide and terrified, because Adam made eye contact and laughed with me to ease my discomfort.

Jimbo the handsome son-of-a-bitch explained. "I hope you're okay with open expressions of man-love and tight tank tops. We get a little freaky in here sometimes." I laughed, unsure of what else to do.

When the interview was over, I checked my phone and, to my surprise, two whole hours had passed in this way. And, also to my surprise, I had fun. This unconventional crew of characters had managed to distract me from my prepared performance with their encouragement to be silly, to be earnest, to just be.

One hour later, Diane called.

"We want you as our public relations specialist. We see how you and Adam connect, and we think you two would make a great team."

3

AN AFFAIR WITH FREEDOM

"Are you a Christian?" asked Chloe, one of my new coworkers, as we ate company-sponsored salads on the landscaped patio out back. Chloe grew up in the church with my husband, so I knew the right answer to her question, the answer I had come up with for myself after years of researching and trying.

"I believe Jesus Christ existed and helped lots of people," I said. "And C.S. Lewis explains how the only options are for him to be 'lunatic, liar or Lord.' He didn't sound like a lunatic, and I don't think he was a liar, so, yeah, I guess he must be Lord."

"I don't believe in God," Chloe said, stopping my fork between plate and face.

"Really?"

"At least not the one of the Bible," she said. "Why would a loving God let children suffer, let them be molested or have illnesses?"

I regurgitated some line I'd heard from the church, about

how this world is relatively insignificant and God has a greater plan.

Chloe went on to present an intelligent and well thought-out argument for the non-existence of God, and while I wasn't sure whether I agreed with everything she said, one thing from our conversation would change my life forever.

I had lied to her about what I believe, and my heart felt a dull ache as I recognized, for the first time, that I felt I had to do that.

"I don't know. It's very cult-ish. Just make sure they don't brainwash you," John said as I packed my bags for the Tony Robbins seminar that my new employer sent all its headquarters employees to.

"It'll be fine. It's not a big deal. It's just a motivational speaker." I told him all the things I'd been telling myself, because actually I was afraid. Chloe and two other coworkers had told me how the Robbins conference completely changed their lives, and I didn't know what a changed life would look like. My current life didn't have room for change, with a marriage approaching its eighth year, a new house under construction, a boat, two cars, a dog, some beige couches.

Walking into the building in San Jose was exhilarating, thousands of people all very different, all colors, ages and sizes, but having something in common, a look of hope in their eyes. They wanted to change their lives, and the energy of six thousand hopers in one place was electric.

A coworker recommended to not sit near anyone you know, because it might inhibit you, so I wedged myself safely among strangers somewhere in the middle of the giant auditorium.

As corny as it all seemed—a massive man running out onto the stage to inspirational music, clapping his hands while diehard fans lost their shit over his presence—I had resolved to give this my all and set aside the skepticism that was my default setting. I jumped up and down with them, for the sake of being involved.

The first day we jumped up and down a lot, and we walked on hot coals while chanting, "Cool moss, cool moss, cool moss." That's about all I remember. Sore feet, cool moss.

The second day we jumped up and down some more, and, about halfway through the day, Tony asked us to engage in something called "The Dickens Process." The exercise asked us to identify our "limiting beliefs." The room became quiet as we turned to our workbooks. While the people around me scribbled furiously, I read the instructions over and over again:

"Identify three limiting beliefs that have been producing unwanted or negative consequences in your life."

Beliefs. Beliefs. My head throbbed with the word, with the concept of believing. What did I believe? My mind went back to that day on the patio, when I had lied to Chloe about being a Christian. Whatever I believed, I certainly didn't feel it was okay to say it.

And that's when it hit me: my limiting belief, the only belief I had for nearly a decade, was that *I had to believe what my husband believed.*

For his approval, for his love, I had to believe all of it. Believe that anyone who hadn't heard about Jesus was going to Hell. Believe that Mexican immigrants are a threat to our jobs. Believe that higher education is an indoctrination tool of the liberal left. Believe that you can never enjoy your work. Believe that exercise sucks, that health consciousness and organics and vegetarianism are for weirdos. Believe that not wanting kids makes you selfish. Believe that going dancing makes you a vapid slut.

I didn't actually believe any of those things that, for ten years now, I had let guide my every action, every decision, every night crying in bed, living a life I didn't want. There, sitting in a metal folding chair, fluorescent lights overhead, surrounded by six thousand people, I sobbed.

I sobbed so hard that snot poured out of my nose, so hard that surely everyone around me heard. I sobbed so hard that I couldn't hold my body up anymore, and I melted into a puddle on the floor where I held my head in my hands and convulsed and sobbed some more. After a while, my sobs subsided into sniffles, I lifted my head from the ground, sat back on my calves, and I felt calm like never before. I felt free, for the first time, to be and believe whatever I wanted.

Ironically, once I stopped forcing myself to believe in my husband's particular way, the wide-open space inside my heart enabled me to feel God's presence more than ever—a presence of pure love and peace that I call by a number of names, so not to lose sight of the ineffable: God, the Source, the Higher Power, the Sage, the Creative, the Universe.

I was so excited about my newfound freedom that I told my coworkers, now friends, about the experience. They hugged me and championed my evolution. But, when I got home, when I walked through the door and saw John sitting on the beige couch, I felt heavy, guilty, as though I'd had an affair with Freedom and surely he'd note the scent of it on my skin, the lust for it in my eyes.

"How was the seminar?" John asked. "Did they brainwash you?"

"It was great. I really liked it."

4

EPHEMERAL

My new supervisor Adam and I sat with two women in an Arizona country bar. We were there to tactfully cut ties with their public relations agency, given my new appointment. As we made small talk with them, Adam threw out the word—ephemeral—with ease, perfectly in context, and it flipped a switch. I hadn't felt attracted to him previously, but the way he used words awoke something in me that I had forgotten and buried long ago.

"Why would you say preposterous when you mean bad?" my husband would criticize. "It's pretentious, and it takes longer." I argued, of course, that preposterous means something different from bad, just as pretentious means something different from pompous. But no matter. I had long since abandoned my passion for prose, knowing it had no audience.

The flight home to Oregon felt like minutes, as Adam and I rode shoulder to shoulder in the far back of the company's private plane, talking about everything from nuances of words to life's purpose.

Nervous and out of practice, I fumbled over words while he massaged them, manipulated them, tossed them in the air like pizza dough and made them into a masterpiece. He used words I had to later look up, and I coveted his eloquence.

So, I felt honored to have the attention of his genius for these few hours, even if he was essentially my hostage here. I wondered if he was getting bored, if he wished he had sat up front with the more interesting people, if he noticed how long I paused before answering, or how I sometimes used big words in the wrong context.

"This has been really nice, talking like this," I said.

"We have great conversations," he said, grinning with golden eyes sparkling. "Let's leave it at that."

I blushed. He thought our conversations were great, too. He liked talking to me, too. He likes me, he likes me, the brilliant one likes me! And wait, leave it at what? Was there somewhere else to leave it?

Adam had never mentioned his wife and kids during the few weeks we had worked together, speaking daily, but another coworker had come into our shared office recently and asked him about them.

Curious, I looked him up on Facebook, only to discover that I knew his wife. She had been my wedding caterer, eight years ago on the Oregon coast. Amazed by the coincidence, I told Adam about it.

"Oh yeah, I was there," he said.

"What?"

"I never go to her work things, but since it was on the coast, we made a weekend of it."

"You were at my wedding? Do you remember it?"

"Yeah, the kids and I were running around the beach."

"Huh. That's so weird."

It felt more than coincidental that this man who now stirred my soul had been present the day I lost it, as though it had flown up on the coastal breeze and landed in his hands.

5

IT'S ALL ABOUT CONTEXT

A dam and I started texting.

It was innocent enough, him asking me about a press release, checking on some work that lingered from the day. Within a couple of weeks, those sporadic texts turned into nightly novels, hours spent volleying back and forth with the speed and skill of Olympic chatter champions.

John sat on the couch, watching TV, and I sat in the armchair across the room, texting with Adam.

ADAM
Have you read On the Road?

ERIN
No, is it a good one?

ADAM
You'll dig it. I'll bring it for you on Monday.

ERIN
Sweet. Have you read every book on the face of the Earth?

ADAM

Not every one. Like 90% ;)

ERIN

Sigh. You make me feel like an ignoramus.

ADAM

Whatever. You're far smarter than me.

ERIN

Smarter than I. Because there is an implied verb, in that you intend to say, 'You're far smarter than I (am).' Hence the need for a subject pronoun. Not object."

ADAM

My intelligence is only a pale reflection of your brilliance.

I laughed out loud. I loved the rare opportunities when I got to correct Adam's grammar. So it was all innocent. Totally innocent. Was it innocent?

"I got fifteen minutes left in me," John said, as he settled on *Seinfeld* and set the remote control on the beige couch arm.

"Okay," I said. I used to try to convince him to stay awake with me, but I had stopped trying.

"How was work today?" He tried.

"It was good."

"I had a really good sandwich today," he said.

"Oh, really? What was it?" I tried.

"Um, let's see." He looked up and to the right, squinting his eyes and thinking. "It had corned beef. Provolone. Mustard." He paused, twisting his mouth. "Deli mustard." He thought some more. "Ah, ham! It had ham."

"Both ham and corned beef?"

"Yeah! It was awesome."

"Sounds good." I looked at my phone. Two new messages.

"And pickles. It also had pickles," he added.

I looked at him and breathed in hard through my nose. "Sounds yummy. We'll have to go there together sometime." I looked at my phone. Seven new messages.

"Can I rub your feet?" John asked. I laid my phone face-down on the chair arm and looked up at him.

"No, I'm okay."

"Can I get you anything?"

"No," I said.

He got up and walked past me to the kitchen. "Can I get you anything to drink?"

"No."

He grabbed a beer, walked back past me, and sat down on the couch. I could feel the burn of him watching me.

"Come on, let me rub your feet."

I looked up and made eye contact for the first time in months. A firm, drop-it-already eye contact. John dropped it, and I felt mean.

"I think I want to read the Quran," I said.

"What? No," he said. "I mean, I just don't think that's a very good idea."

"I think it would be interesting," I said. "To understand other religions, what they believe."

"That stuff, that Islam stuff, is fucked up." He kept watching the TV. "You don't want that polluting your mind."

"Did you know that they believe certain parts of the Bible? There are actually more parallels than people think. I think that's so interesting, like maybe it's all essentially the same truth but from different cultural perspectives, with different semantics." I wondered if he knew what semantics meant.

"Well I don't wanna read anything by a bunch of towel heads who wanna kill us," he said, starting to channel surf again. I looked at my phone. Eleven messages.

"You want me to leave the TV on?" he asked, precisely fifteen minutes from his initial warning.

"No, that's alright." I couldn't stand the constant drone of the same sitcoms playing every night, all night, in the living room, in the bedroom, filling the time and space with anything but us.

"You coming to bed?" he asked.

"I'm not tired. I think I'll stay up a bit longer."

"Come cuddle with me."

"In a bit, honey," I said, making eye contact. I resumed my text conversation, and, as John walked behind my chair, heading for the bedroom, I felt my cheeks burn with shame. But I wasn't doing anything wrong, was I?

I had recently started to read *The I Ching or Book of Changes*, an ancient Chinese book of wisdom that Tony Robbins had recommended. (I, apparently, had joined the cult.) Once John was in bed, I opened up the *I Ching* app to consult the oracle for my daily reading. In ancient China, they would shake three coins in their hands, drop them, and, based on how the coins fell, they would draw hexagrams that indicated which chapters to read, and, consequently, what areas of your life needed attention and reform.

The app made this whole process easier, requiring only six little taps on the coin images on the screen. It returned, "Fellowship With Others," and one paragraph stood out:

"The fundamental rule of the *I Ching* for the conduct of
relationships is that they take place in the open. This
means that every facet of a relationship should be seen
as fair and correct by *everyone* concerned, not just yourself. It also means that it is improper to enter into or
continue in relationships with unspoken reservations or
hidden intentions."[1]

No, I wasn't doing anything wrong, talking about literature and shared interests with a male friend. I was *feeling*
something wrong, and, with each day, it was getting harder
to hide it.

---

1. *The I Ching* English translation by Brian Browne Walker.

6

FUCKED-UP FORMULA

Adam swayed in too close to my mouth and pointed to the door of the office where he conducted my interview six months earlier.

"We were meant to meet in there," he said. An empty bottle of Maker's Mark whisky sat on the table, and we stood beneath the only pale light in a big open room, left empty by all our coworkers several hours ago.

"What do you mean?" I knew exactly what he meant, but I wanted him to say it. For once and for all, stop implying, stop dancing, stop alluding, stop texting and fucking say it.

He laughed. "*We* are going to be alright, Erin." The way he said *we* ping-ponged around my head. *We* as colleagues? *We* as best friends? *We* as a couple, forever and ever?

"I can't decide if you've got it all figured out or if you're as fucked up as I am," I said, hoping he might answer.

"I think you know the answer to that." His phone rang, and he silenced it. I admitted that I, too, had missed several calls. Taking that as our cue, we walked outside together, into the winter air, and while I usually hate the cold, I didn't feel it.

He put his hands in his pockets and swayed from side to side. He leaned in close to my ear, and I could feel the hot energy from his scruffy cheek burning mine.

"You're the smartest chick I know," he said. I used to hate the way he said Californian things like "chick," or "bro," but I had seen how such colloquial quirks were an attempt to play down a vast intelligence that had me swooning upon its revelation.

So, that night, I wanted him to keep whispering in my ear, tickling my face with his five o'clock shadow. I wanted him to keep telling me flattering things. I wanted him to grab me by the arms and kiss my mouth hard with his mouth that would taste smoky and his tongue that moved fast, captivating a room whenever he spoke. But I stepped back. Not because he was drunk, or because he was more than a decade my senior, or even because he was married. I stepped back, because I was married.

"I'd better go," I said.

He leaned back, grinning, eyes glazed over, and I still wonder what could have happened, had I not retreated. As in a dream, where you don't know how you get from one place to the next, I was climbing into my car and he into his. Before he got in, he looked at me over the roof of his car and yelled, "I love you. You're awesome."

I shut my car door and placed my hands on the cold steering wheel, pushing my spine against the seat back. He said it. Drunkenly, he said it, but he said it. "I love you, too," I said, out loud but unheard. I meant it more than ever before in my life.

Everything in my life until now could be explained by

logic, added up in a spreadsheet and sorted into neat columns. I married John because he was a nice guy who loved me. I went to University of Oregon because in-state school was more affordable. I studied advertising because there were lots of marketing jobs in the paper that year. We bought property because it was a buyer's market. We settled in Southern Oregon because it was near our families. I went to church because good people go to church. I loved middle-aged, unstable, married-with-kids coworker Adam Campbell because I loved him, and nothing about it made sense or fit into my perfect-life formula.

I tried to stop loving Adam. I even made a list of everything to not love about him, like the way his hair was intentionally messy. The way he wore shorts in winter and beanies in summer. The way he rambled on talking forever and loved the sound of his own voice. I tried to hate his crinkling eyes and loping gait. But the truth was, I loved all those things.

At the same time, I tried to love John. I planned him a big thirtieth surprise birthday party, with all his friends and family present. We went away for the weekend to Portland, where we enjoyed romantic dinners and comedy shows and walked through the city holding hands. For Valentine's Day, I sat in the front seat of his pick-up truck and tried to write him a love letter. I sat there, in the early morning light, staring at a blank page resting on the steering wheel.

Dear John,
You have always been there for me…

I crumpled it up and started again.

Dear John,
After all these years...

This was the part where I was supposed to say, "I love you," or, "I wouldn't want anyone but you," or, "You're my best friend." But I couldn't. I loved Adam, I wanted Adam, and Adam was my best friend.

Months earlier, I had tried to talk to John about what was missing. One night, as we stood facing the bathroom mirror, completing our evening routine for the three-thousandth time, I spontaneously began to sob, choking on foamy tooth-paste as spittle dribbled down my chin.

"What's wrong sweetheart?" he asked. "What's wrong?"

"I need to have fun with you," I eked out. "I'm meeting all these people at my new job and I'm having fun with them, but I need to have fun with you."

"I know. I'm sorry, sweetheart. I've just been working so much. We'll have fun. I'll try harder. We'll have fun together."

But nothing changed. I don't blame John for that. We had been together so long that neither of us knew how to change for the other. Together we were like two oxen yoked with the burden of expectation, and there was no room for me to veer left toward self-discovery or for him to veer right toward whatever it was he needed.

I thought back to *The I Ching*'s advice, "that it is improper to enter into or continue in relationships with unspoken reservations or hidden intentions." I could not change my feelings, so, now, it was time to change my situation.

I watched the clock. John would be home any time now. How do you tell someone after eight years of marriage, after ten years together, that you don't want to do this anymore?

I looked around our perfect home that he and his dad finished building just in time for Christmas. Perfect appliances I researched for days. Perfect throw pillows that weren't too floral. Perfect-shade-of-gray wall that took many trials and errors. Perfect wooden bench that made our entry look like *Better Homes & Gardens*. Perfect hand-painted shower curtain. Perfect dog sleeping by the fireplace. Everything was perfect, and I didn't want any of it (except the dog).

With no idea how to move forward, I got on my knees and prayed for the right words to say. When John walked in through the front door that evening, no words were needed. I felt a surprising calm, and he looked at me with a knowing that we hadn't shared in a long time, maybe ever. It was as though he was really seeing me, and he saw that I was finished, with us, with this life. He saw what he had been trying not to see for a long time.

"I was like an ostrich with my head in the sand," he said.

"I don't even know what I believe," I told him. "I need to be free to explore that, to figure it out."

"I'll let you do that. I can let you do that," he said, grasping at what was already gone.

"But *I* can't do that when I'm with you. I know you so well that I already know everything you're thinking, every judgment firing inside your head."

I had never thought of John as controlling, with his mild-mannered nature and gentle admonitions that seemed rooted in rational concern.

"I don't think you should be friends with her; she's not a

good influence," he once said of a brilliant, liberal college friend whom I adored. So I stopped hanging out with her.

"I've seen how drinking can lead people down a bad path," he would say. So I didn't touch a drop of alcohol (until he started drinking, and then it became acceptable for me, too).

"Of course she left her husband after she got that boob job," he criticized, often implying that any boost in self-confidence turns women into abandoning harlots.

I later understood that he did control me, a chronic people-pleaser, with my greatest fear: the looming threat of disapproval.

John agreed to a trial separation, which I think we both knew was a softened step on the way to divorce. I moved out within the month, into a house nearby with two girlfriends from work, Jen and Kara.

I had told John the truth, about needing freedom to express and find myself. I omitted the little detail about being in love with another man. But I was not leaving because I thought I could be with Adam. At that time, he was away on a happy holiday with his wife and kids. We hadn't talked in a bit, given my recommitment efforts, and I believed that our relationship would never be more than that of supervisor and subordinate, mentor and pupil, rock star and groupie. I adored him, but he simply humored me. Or so I thought.

7

TWO LIES AND A TRUTH

T he following week, back at work, I found three sheets of paper face-down on my desk. I smiled as no girl has ever smiled before. He remembered.

Before Adam left on vacation, we had discussed doing a writing exercise. We were holed up in the conference room one afternoon, working on rewriting website content, when I came across an old version of copy and laughed.

"You wrote this one," I said, holding up the print-out.

He grinned in that way that made his eyes squinty and sparkly. "I did. How'd you know?"

"It's too good. All the others are shit."

He laughed. "They are shit, aren't they?"

"And besides, I can hear your voice. I know your style."

"Yeah, I'm pretty sure I know yours, too."

"Do you? I didn't know I had a style," I said, really hoping I had a style. All I'd written for the past ten years were press releases, academic essays and business articles. Creative writing was but a distant memory of my youth, once profuse with poetry, prose and passion.

"I'm certain I could pick it out of a line-up," he said.

"That's an interesting idea. Why don't we do that?"

"Like two lies and a truth," he said, knowing, as usual, precisely what I was getting at. "One piece of your writing and two pieces from other sources. Due the Monday I get back from vacation."

So here we were, back from break, ready to share. My hand trembled as I handed over the homework. I hadn't shown anyone my creative writing since I was a girl. I felt so vulnerable, submitting my unworthy work to his esteemed eyes. It was, for me, an intimacy deeper than that of exposing the physical body.

We sat at our desks and read in silence.

His first piece was about a man driving fast and contemplating crashing and committing suicide. The second piece I can't recall; it was so mediocre I knew it wasn't his. The third piece was about a middle-aged man who was dreadfully unhappy in his suburban marriage with his dull wife who didn't understand his metaphors, whom he said 'I love you' to but whom it was obvious he actually despised. It was the best of the three, and I knew that it was his. I also knew that the man in the story was him.

Adam held up one of my pages. "This one is yours."

"Yes," I said, pleased that he did recognize my voice in a short poem about a metaphorical snowscape. "This one is yours." I held up the autobiographical piece.

"Yep. How did you know?"

"I vacillated between the suicide one and this one, but I knew it was yours once I saw the word 'clever.' You love that word."

"Damn. I'm so predictable."

I laughed. "And clever."

We decided to continue the exchange, turning in one page of writing to one another every day, editing each other's work in the afternoons over a glass of whisky on the rocks. The writing exchange was my joy, my whole reason for getting up in the morning. I craved his red-pen bloodshed upon my pages, with the most insightful edits I'd ever received and just enough flattery to keep me encouraged. "You're a good writer," he would affirm. "You're meant for more than writing press releases in Southern Oregon."

In equal measure, I looked forward to seeing his story unfold, my heart jumping with every twist, every revelation that I perceived as a window into the home life he never discussed:

On day one, his protagonist Abe resented the stupidity of his shallow wife.

On day two, Abe had an intimate affair with a younger coworker called Sophie.

On day five, Abe resented his wife, again.

On day nine, Abe and Sophie stayed late at the office, exchanging witty banter and drinking whisky.

On day ten, Abe masturbated to the thought of Sophie and rejected his wife's advances

On day fourteen, Abe described Sophie as a "fire to play with," something to make his boring suburban life more interesting. (On day fourteen, Erin cried.)

On day sixteen, Sophie disappeared. The scenes were no longer about Sophie.

On day nineteen, the writing disappeared. When I got to the office that morning, there was no page face-down on my desk.

"Where's your writing?" I asked, sensing something was

amiss. "You were bragging yesterday about getting it done first, so where is it?"

He looked across our desks, which we had pushed together last week, like children pushing their beds together at a sleepover. His eyes were impenetrable, his voice cold and flat. "I'm gonna have to discontinue that project."

Those words created in my heart and stomach a physical effect so sickening, so painful, that I have never since doubted that these vibrational frequencies traveling upon air can land a knock-out punch more excruciating than any fist or weapon. I got up and stepped through the sliding glass door to the office balcony, the one where he and I had shared many words and many cigarillos (which I'd begun smoking, to spend more time with him).

I was glad the blinds were closed, as I slid down the glass and sat on the deck, cradling my knees in my arms. I didn't cry so much as yelp, a puppy-like whimper wheezing out of my chest and escaping without my consent. "Ow," I whimpered. "Ow, ow, ow."

Surely soon he would come outside to talk about it. Surely soon he would explain the reason. Surely soon he would arrive with one page in hand, saying he was sorry and that it was silly to ever have considered stopping something that was so important to both of us. But he never came. Like Sophie, Erin disappeared, condemned once again to a meaningless nothing without Adam to write and acknowledge her character.

After most of our colleagues had left for the day, I swiveled my chair toward him.

"Do you want me to ask?"

"If you want," he said, his usual grin a grimace.

"What happened?"

He exhaled pure misery. "A long, unexpected conversation." I knew that this conversation had been with his wife, and I knew that she must have found something. He held his head in his hands. "I'm fucked up."

For once, we didn't talk, because there was nothing more to say. I already knew the whole story, from his few utterances, and I had no choice in the matter.

"Will you keep writing?" I asked, my primary concern. He had been so proud of himself, like a little boy, every day, eyes lit up, going on about how this was the most progress he had ever made toward completing a manuscript and how it felt really good to be doing something that mattered.

"No," he said, like a beaten, cowering street dog. "I can't."

"Do you want a drink?" I asked, opening the whisky drawer.

"No," he said. "I can't. I'm on the wagon, like Eddie."

Our friend and coworker Eddie's wife had insisted he stop drinking a couple of weeks ago. I tried to make eye contact, that deep recognition of one another's beings that so fulfilled me, but his eyes were now shallow and closed to connection.

"I hope you keep writing, though," he said.

"I will," I said, outwardly determined, inwardly terrified.

———

That night, I sat on the couch with my laptop, in the house that I now shared with Kara and Jen, my coworkers and close friends. "Day 20," I typed at the top of the blank page, which returned a blinking cursor, threatening me, heckling me.

Write something, you idiot, it blinked. *Just write something. Can't you do it? No, you can't do it. Not without him, you can't do it. You're worthless. You'll never be a writer,* it blinked, and I sobbed.

I was more of an occasional-piña-colada girl before I met Adam, but now I was frequent whisky. I went to the kitchen and rifled through the cupboard, which produced a half bottle of vodka. I added lemonade directly to the bottle, sat on the floor, leaned up against the couch and started drinking, at 5 p.m. By the time my roommates came home an hour later, I think vodka came out in my tears.

"Sweetheart, what's wrong?" Jen said, as she sat on one side of me and Kara sat down on the other.

"He stopped writing," I sputtered, falling over into the fetal position with my head on Kara's knee. She held me while they spoke sweet assurances and stroked my hair.

8

A LITTLE BIRD TOLD ME

At work the next day, I expected Adam to ignore me, but he talked to me more than ever. He asked me to go out back for multiple cigarillo breaks, and we both neglected our work to spend time together. It was Thursday, and we had to get our fill before the three-day, textless weekend.

The weekend was lonely. He went camping with his family, and, not hearing a word from him, I imagined him patching up his failing marriage and falling in love all over again.

Sunday night, unable to sleep, with work looming in three hours, I received a tweet notification. Adam, who seldom engaged in social media expressions, had tweeted:

Behind her eyes there's curtains. -pj

It was Pearl Jam, our shared favorite band. I immediately Googled the lyrics.

Parting Ways
Behind her eyes there's curtains,
And they've been closed to hide the flames, remains.
She knows their future's burning, but she can smile just
    the same.
And though her mood is fine today,
There's a fear they'll soon be parting ways.

After I read the lyrics, my heart surged with hope. He is going to leave her! This is his way of letting me know! After three torturous days alone with her and no intellectual stimulation, he must be ready to call it quits. I fell asleep with ease and got up with excitement, ready to see him and talk about this major decision.

But he never discussed anything of the sort with me. Instead, a profusion of cryptic tweets came my way that I hungrily tried to decipher, looking up lyrics and agonizing over their meaning. After one week of this tweet torture, he texted me.

ADAM

What are you up to?

ERIN

You can talk to me now?

ADAM

I just don't see why I can't talk to my best friend.

I swallowed, and though I didn't want to ask, I asked.

ERIN

Shouldn't your wife be your best friend?

ADAM

I put those things in separate categories.

I accepted the weak explanation, exultant to have my best friend back. The famine turned into feast once more, texting all day, every day. We hardly slept most nights, and, in the morning, at work, we went outside and talked some more. Within a couple weeks, we resumed the writing exchange.

9

THE EVIL ELLIPSIS

I watched the little ellipsis dance. Three gray dots, doing the worm at the bottom of my iPhone screen, carrying on their round backs an entire world of either happiness or despair. What would he say? It disappeared.

I knew he'd received my text. *Seen 10:32 a.m.*, the iPhone tattled.

The ellipsis began its teasing, devilish dance again, and I held my breath hoping for the words I wanted him to say. Something like, "I love you," or, "I need you," or, "I can't live without you."

It disappeared again. I waited. I began to type, and I backspaced, so he could see my ellipsis, too, and know that I was waiting. He was thinking so much, when the answer should be simple.

I read the last text I sent to him once more.

ERIN

> If you told me today, 100% conclusively that we were only going to be friends and that's all we'd ever be, then I would have no choice but to move on and make myself forget. But you haven't done that. Can you do that?

ADAM

. . .

After five minutes watching, waiting, for the text my whole heart hinged upon, I began to look for him online, in the numerous virtual worlds where we engaged:

Twitter: not a tweet or retweet since 4:32 p.m. yesterday.

Skype: no green dot showing he was online.

Words With Friends: no words played.

Email: nothing since our last writing exchange.

Facebook: no green dot there, either; last log-in twenty-three hours ago.

Her **Facebook:** as usual, there was no trace of him there, either, but I still checked, to torture myself.

I tapped back into our text exchange and scrolled up to the top, to read it from the beginning again.

ADAM

> Regardless of where we are, we know where we need to be. Or I'm just going to keep causing you pain.

ERIN

> Do I cause you pain? Is this one-sided? Be honest.

Oh, how I wanted to cause him pain, how I wanted his heart to ache for me the way that mine did for him. They say that if you really love, you never want any harm to befall your beloved. While this may be true of "normal" love, I here attest that, in unrequited love, the case is quite the opposite. One begins to associate suffering with loving and, therefore, you begin to believe that the former begets the latter. If I can make him suffer, I can make him *understand* that he loves me.

ADAM

It's not one-sided.

ERIN

We're still going to be friends, no matter what happens, okay?

ADAM

Again. That, Erin, is what I don't want messed up. Under any circumstance.

ERIN

You express such concern that it will be ruined. What do you think is going to ruin it?

ADAM

Oh, feelings have a tendency to eff stuff up.

I've seen in others, the feelings of frustration lead to bitterness, and it's terribly sad.

I want to insure that never happens.

ERIN

The way you will do that is to be upfront about what expectations should be.

ADAM

The expectation is that nothing really changes. Only the acknowledgment of what can be and the peace we have knowing it.

ERIN

Okay. If that is what you want, and you are sure in that, then I'll make peace with it.

ADAM

Can you do that? Is it possible?

ERIN

Can you?

ADAM

Truthfully? Not overnight. No.

ERIN

So you tell me you have feelings, and you know that they can't just be turned off...So, I have to ask: what is your game plan?

ADAM

Haha.

ERIN

Deny deny deny? Ignore ignore ignore?

Is that the right way?

ADAM

Are you kidding? I have no idea.

I am lost, I'm no guide. But I am by your side. #pj

ERIN

All I know is, I try to forget. I have tried really, really hard to forget.

And something won't let me.

ADAM

I understand.

Totally.

I still felt so confused. I rubbed the side of my neck, and my right eye began to twitch. If he only wanted to be friends, why was he touching my knee beneath tables or the small of my back as we entered parties? Why was he texting me morning and night, telling me I was a smart and beautiful woman? Was I crazy? Was this normal friend behavior, and I had taken it and twisted it and totally misunderstood? I recalled his stabbing comment a couple of weeks ago, when I tried to inquire about his intentions: "You see what you want to see." My eye twitched again.

And then, the ellipsis. The damned dancing devil of an ellipsis. I watched it like an expectant dog watches her ball, flinching upon any minor movement. Then, after what seemed an eternity, he wrote.

ADAM

Yes.

Yes! He said yes! A yes is always a good thing, is it not? But as fast as my heart rose, it fell, as I realized what that yes was actually saying: Yes, friends are all we would ever be.

ERIN

Yes, you are telling me that now?

An infatuated fool, I still couldn't believe it. After all we had shared. After all he had said. After all he had typed, texted, tweeted.

ADAM

Yes.

ERIN

Okay. Thank you.

It hurts like hell, but at least it's clear.

Just don't change your mind.

Which it sounds like you won't, now. You said it certainly.

ADAM

It does hurt. :(

ERIN

That's the kind of stuff that makes me feel like you're not certain. But if you're telling me you are, I will trust that...

ADAM

I do need you trust me. But I also want you to know that I have feelings at stake, too

ERIN

Well geez, if that isn't a contradiction...

ADAM

What, feelings?

ERIN

No, I'm just so confused. Spinning. I'm sorry :(

ADAM

Don't be sorry.

Have you ever wanted to hurt your best friend?

So, that's what hurts.

That's what I'm doing.

ERIN

You'd hurt me more if you weren't honest.

So there it is.

It's okay.

As long as you are sure, then I trust you.

ADAM

Trust me.

The firmness and finality of those last two words hit me like a shotput ball to the sternum. That was it, the end, the 100% certain and conclusive end.

TO HAVE LOVED

W hy they gave the two of us our own rental car, I'll never know. There were suspicions surrounding our relationship, and, yet, the company president decided that he and our other four colleagues would cram into one car while Adam and I took our own. But perhaps everything was supposed to work out serendipitously that day.

We were supposed to meet with a Portland tech company to discuss the development of an app, but, despite having an appointment, no one answered the phone. A more diligent pair might have driven to the office, pounded on the door and screamed, "Let me in, godammit, we have work to do!" But Adam and I didn't do any of this. We stopped off at a bar for drinks.

"Do you think it's better to have loved and lost than never to have loved at all?" he asked, a standard beginning to one of our drawn-out, philosophical conversations that I so treasured.

"I do," I said, without hesitating.

"I don't know that I do."

"You think it's better to not have loved?" I asked.

"Sometimes, I think it's better not to know what you're missing out on."

"I think it's better to love, because at least then you recognize your heart's full potential. Why would you want to live your life without experiencing the depth of your emotions?"

"Is it good to experience the extremes? Isn't it better to be balanced?" he asked.

I took a drink of my third beer in that sitting. "You know that we both aren't very good at balance."

"Once again, you're right." He laughed. I loved that laugh.

We talked for a couple of hours, for the first time free from the eyes of leering coworkers, and it felt good, too good. It felt like the best day of my life.

"You know," he said with a cheeky look in his eyes, "Powell's is just around the corner."

Powell's is a huge, multi-level bookstore with a collection to rival any library in the world, with an entire room dedicated to antique, first-edition classics. We got up, paid, and ran the three blocks to Powell's.

We walked up and down the abandoned aisles, running our fingertips along the books, feeling them, smelling them, ingesting their antiquity into our souls. We ogled the first editions. We stood close to one another, feeling each other's breaths, energies, hanging in the air and desiring to dance. I don't know if it was me or the books, but Adam got a huge boner.

"We better go," he said. "The others will be waiting for us at the airport."

When we got into our rental car, his boner was still there, and the combination of the alcohol, hormones and burning love turned me into a woman I'd not known before. Once cardigans, ponytails and prudence, I became a seductress.

I wore a low-cut top with a push-up bra and a tight miniskirt. Thinking back now, I can't believe I wore such a thing for a business meeting, but a mind fed by desire doesn't always make the best decisions, in dress or deed. My wardrobe over the past year had become increasingly sparse.

As he drove, I put one high-heeled foot up on the glove box. I will never forget how he looked at me then, with a desire in his eyes that could burn through steel. He reached over and grabbed my hand. This was all the invitation I needed. I moved onto my knees, leaned across the center console, and began to tongue the lobe of his ear as I had imagined myself doing so many times. His rapid, shallow breaths were my reward.

"We can't do this," Adam said, as he put his hand on my upper thigh. I unzipped his pants. "We have to be so careful," he said, looking for a place to pull over.

"Fuck," he said, still driving. "We're stuck in the fucking airport loop. I can't think." He drove around in circles, passing the exit again and again as his brain high on hormones couldn't pay attention long enough to watch for the sign. Or maybe he was stalling.

As we went around the airport loop a third time, I began to think of how he would feel if he did this with me, how he would go home to his wife and feel guilty. I zipped his pants back up. As it turns out, I loved him more than I wanted him.

"I don't think I've ever had anyone zip my pants *up* before," he said.

I settled back in my seat, and we parked in front of the private airport terminal where the company jet waited. He grabbed my hand and looked me in the eyes.

"Look, Erin, this would've happened by now if it weren't for my kids. I really dig you."

Ouch. I flashed back to a nosy coworker's brutal admonition a couple of months prior: "Adam digs you. He doesn't love you." I'd received a similar warning from my roommate Kara: "I think you might be more invested in this than he is."

It's true, I had seen him make that same piercing eye contact with other women around the office; it stung each time I caught it in my periphery. I had even seen, over Kara's shoulder one evening, that he also sent her a flirtatious, after-hours text. She promised it was a one-off thing, and I filed it and the other red flags under insignificant-when-it-comes-to-the-love-of-my-life.

"Let's have a smoke before the flight," I said, getting out of the car and pulling down my skirt. We leaned up against the building, both exhausted from the adrenaline and hormone rush.

"I have to do what is best for my kids," he explained, but I was preoccupied. *I dig you. I dig you. I dig you.* I heard the words over and over again as we puffed on the same cigarillo.

"I love you." I sang it like a jazz song, desperate to make the truth known so there could be no more confusion about my feelings or intentions. "I love you."

"I love you, too..." he said, like a question. Weak where his voice was normally strong, tapering off at the end where sincerity would naturally inflect. It was the 'I love you' that said, 'I don't love you.'

NO PLACE LIKE HOME

I quit my job, and I booked a ticket to Cusco, Peru, where I had been happy once and hoped I might be happy again. I couldn't stand to see Adam, to love him every day and know that he would not love me in return.

It's a writer's curse that you have to do everything in the most dramatic way possible. It makes for a more compelling narrative in your head. I couldn't just move to Portland and get a new PR job. I had to abandon life as I knew it and move to a third-world country, alone.

I had planned a dramatic all-out exit from the marketing agency, cutting off all contact with Adam, but there was this little detail of income to consider. So, when the company generously offered to let me work remotely from Peru for three months a year, so long as I worked from Oregon the other nine months, I had to accept.

In the taxi, the driver peppered me in Spanish with the usual slew of questions. Where are you from? What do you do? Why are you here? How old are you? Are you married?

"I'm divorced," I told him. I had received the official dissolution judgment days before my departure.

"Did he hit you?" he asked, his red-rimmed eyes wide with horror.

"No," I responded, blushing with shame that John didn't hit me. Maybe I didn't have a valid reason to leave. Maybe finding myself and peace for my soul and self-expression and all that nonsense were luxuries for spoiled girls who didn't know a hard day's work, driving taxi twelve hours a day to support twelve children. I decided not to tell Peruvian people I was divorced anymore.

I was headed for the orphanage, the one place that ever felt like home. I couldn't wait to recreate the happiness I felt five years before. Every day, I would finish teaching the boys English at Noon, and then the eighteen of us would sit down together around a rickety, disintegrating table for lunch. We would pass carefully portioned bowls of yucca soup or lentils and rice down the line, and one of the boys would mumble a shy prayer.

"Dios bendiga esta comida y a mis hermanos en Cristo." *God bless this food and my brothers and sisters in Christ.*

Afterward, we'd play, either drawing or dancing or playing *fútbol*. The kids loved to show me their tricks and talents that earned them a few Peruvian *soles* on the street. They would even show me their techniques for pick-pocketing tourists. I loved them, my scrappy, sweet and needy street kids.

Over the last five years, I had searched PDX to CUZ hundreds of times. I had talked with Peruvian friends on Facebook, promising I would return one day. I had cried in the arms of a stranger at a work conference, confessing that all I wanted was to be back there again. I had pictured this moment, how glorious it would be. How six-year-old Romeo would come running to give me a sticky, candy-mouthed kiss on the cheek. How nineteen-year-old Elías would beat me at chess and show me his latest paintings.

Finally, I was here, on the doorstep of my dream. What used to be a simple, single-story home with colorful, kid-painted murals on the outside wall was now a three-story cement monolith, painted an obnoxious cobalt blue, towering over the modest brick and adobe homes that surrounded it.

I wiped happy tears, pressed the doorbell and waited. Soon, a few of the kids would come running to throw open the door and wrap their arms around my neck, always excited to meet a new visitor or old friend. I waited a minute, and I pushed the doorbell again.

A complicated process of clanking and unlocking proceeded behind the metal door, and a thin, young Peruvian man peered out at me from a dark room.

"Hi!" I said. "I volunteered here five years ago. I know such a long time, and I came back!"

"I'm Herbert," he said, unimpressed. Herbert led me into a dark garage and up a flight of cement stairs, each step heavy and quiet, to the second floor.

I looked around, recognizing nothing. Where there once had been an open-air courtyard with a garden, a clothesline, makeshift soccer goals and a flea-bitten cat called Batman, now there were only pristine polished floors and closed doors.

"Is Romeo here?" I asked. He would be eleven now.

"No, he left about two months ago to live with his mom," Herbert told me. "He was making trouble, stealing."

I worried. Maybe I should have been happy to hear that

Romeo was with his mom, but many of these boys were here precisely because their moms and dads weren't nice. I thought of Romeo's six little toes on each foot, his rotting teeth, his scabies and his sweet dimples.

"And Elías?" When I met Elías, he was nineteen, still residing there as a tutor and loving big brother to the little ones. He had been raised at the shelter, brought in off the streets at the age of twelve, with lice in his waistband and scars on his body.

"Elías had some problems and got kicked out."

"Problems?" I parroted, not really asking but expressing my disappointment. Wasn't this supposed to be a shelter for the scarred, the lonely, the "problems" who once wandered the cold streets of Cusco? What was this if not a place for those "problems"?

I walked into the only open room, a stark, clean classroom filled with uniformed kids working on their homework. Where were my kids? Where were my rough-around-the-edges, sharp-tongued, sweet-hearted boys who came running to steal a much-needed hug? These were not the same kids. Of course, I knew they wouldn't be the same kids. Many of the ones I taught before were now adults, some with kids of their own. But these were not the same kids.

The kids I knew were not quiet or focused. The kids I knew would be pushing each other, calling each other names, pulling their shirts over their heads and talking trash, kicking one another beneath the table. I loved those kids.

And this was not the same place, where we once came together in a yellow-walled classroom, laughing and hugging and sharing soup. My home was gone.

THE CUSCO EVERY-NIGHT LIFE

"**B**rendan?" I knocked on the bedroom door of my nineteen-year-old American house mate. We both rented rooms from a Peruvian, Christian family I had met five years ago, while doing mission work with John.

An exchange student from Kentucky, Brendan had a big build and an even bigger personality. He made us all laugh with his flamboyant accent and mannerisms that made us presume he was gay, until we saw him dry-humping girls in dark corners of night clubs. Brendan could take shots with me on Saturdays and praise *Cristo* on Sundays, no conflict felt.

"Hey there angel! Come on in," Brendan said as he opened the door and shimmied back to his place on the bed.

I joined him there, and he reached into his nightstand to present a box of Clos, the cheapest, boxed white wine that we illicitly chugged out of view of our conservative host parents.

"Are you going out tonight?" I asked. It was Tuesday.

"Oh, you know it." He pushed his lips out to one side,

blinking his dark curly lashes. "And you better come with us. Girlll, you look like you need a night out."

"Yeah, I do. I'll go, just for a bit."

That "bit" turned into me and Brendan's crew of nineteen-year-old friends dancing on the bar barefoot at Mama Africa, one of Cusco's wild hot spots located in the central Plaza de Armas.

Bartenders poured alcohol straight down our throats as we grinded up against one another like stripper poles. *Look at me. Look at me. Please look at me and assure me that I exist and am important and am beautiful.*

Brendan was at his post by the artificial palm tree, humping away, and we girls were getting so sloppy drunk that some of us dropped off the bar like dead flies into the crowd. I'm not sure if I was one of these flies, because I blacked out and only recall Brendan pulling me by the arm from the bathroom (men's or women's, I'm not sure) and saying that they had been looking for me a long time.

This was the beginning of many such drunken nights, as I strained to black out the pain. The pain of 'trust me,' the pain of 'I [don't] love you,' but most of all, the pain of thinking I knew what was real and understanding, for the first time, that everything I knew was wrong.

After another night of blackout drinking, I rolled over and realized I wasn't in my bed when I saw a muscular naked back and ass. I sat up and looked around. A small room, no windows, a sheetless bed, a naked man. Where were we? Peruvian prison? I looked for my phone.

I checked my purse, my clothes, his drawers, his clothes.

I checked under the bed, in the bed, in the bathroom. I panicked not for my safety but for the potentially missed messages from the one I wished were in that bed beside me.

Adam and I still texted constantly. Staying on with the marketing agency allowed Adam a line into my life that I had intended to sever. He started by checking on press releases and, within short order, we were back to the intimate conversations I couldn't quit. My childhood friend Bri had asked me, when I told her I was leaving the country, "How will traveling thousands of miles away fix anything if you haven't detached from him in your heart?" Touché. I was more entrenched in infatuation than ever.

I grabbed the muscled shoulder and shook, afraid to see what, and whom, I'd done. Muscles rolled over and at least was shockingly handsome, a Peruvian Machu Picchu guide I had connected with at a rock concert the night before. He grinned a big white smile and reached up to caress my chin with his thumb and index finger.

"Have you seen my iPhone?" I asked.

"No, you didn't have it with you when we met."

"Are you sure? It was in a bright green case."

"Yeah, I'm sure." He leaned up on an elbow and laughed. "It's just a phone."

I went to shower, but there was no soap. I went to dry off, but there was no towel. I went to pee, but there was no toilet paper. I got dressed in last night's clothes and walked barefoot to the sidewalk where my one-night stand helped me hail a taxi.

"Cuídate," he said. *Take care.* He shut the door behind me, and I let my head fall hard and hungover against the window, staring out at kids playing barefoot soccer and pregnant moms laughing with babies on their hips.

Where I had only slept with two people up until age twenty-eight, my post-divorce numbers were climbing quickly as I desperately pursued a connection to override my inconvenient feelings for Adam. But it hadn't been working out so well.

The first person I slept with was a friend about my age, also divorced, and I told him afterward that I hadn't climaxed.

"Really? Every other woman I've slept with has."

Brand new to single-girl world, I didn't scoff out loud as I should have done. I thought something must be wrong with me and tried to make up for it by being sexier, louder, and then by giving him a massage afterward to somehow make up for my inadequacy.

"You're a real people-pleaser," he observed, and I hoped that, with my star performance, he might not talk badly about me to our mutual friends.

The second guy pulled the line, "It just doesn't feel good to me with a condom." A more confident woman might have said, "Well, guess we aren't having sex tonight." But instead, ever approval-seeking and losing confidence with each encounter, I gave in to this unfair and unsafe request.

The third, a horrific kisser from Spain, satisfied his own need with record speed then threw my panties at me. When I commented on the one-sidedness of the experience, he acted offended. How dare I not appreciate the ten-second usage of his glorious member?

It's hard to share these things, but I know I'm not the first woman they have happened to. I know that we as women are often made to feel as though we had better perform to porn-star perfection in the bedroom, even if the guy is mediocre and inattentive. I never could have imagined that the next person I chose to sleep with would be the most mediocre and inattentive of all.

Every day I rode the *combi,* a ten-passenger van packed with twenty, an hour to the Cusco center for good WiFi. Sometimes I wrote press releases for my company. Mostly, I wrote Adam.

ADAM
Good news, girl.

ERIN
What is it?

ADAM
You'll never guess.

ERIN
I don't want to guess. Tell me.

ADAM
Aw, that's no fun.

ERIN
We both know I'm fun. Tell me.

ADAM
We're going to Honduras.

ERIN
What? Who's going?

Before I left, Adam and I had been coordinating a TV project for a client, and it looked like things were moving ahead. I watched his ellipsis as always: anxious dog, suspended ball. I think he dragged it out on purpose, to make me crazy.

ADAM

You and me. (And Don and Mark.) They want us all there.

ERIN

Shut. Up.

When?

ADAM

At the beginning of October.

ERIN

That's next week!

ADAM

These show biz types move fast.

He wasn't kidding. Little more than a week later, I waited in the lobby of the Tegucigalpa Marriott, wearing my best dress with high heels and holding a silly little welcome sign for the company president, the vice president, and my love.

13

A CURIOSITY

I thought he would touch my face. In the story Adam wrote, at the moment of consummation of the drawn-out, emotional affair, his protagonist Abe reaches up and tenderly strokes Sophie's cheek. This was not like the story.

After a long day of filming then a late dinner with the crew, Adam and I walked out to the pool area for one more drink. We sat close to one another on the concrete patio, light reflections from the pool dancing across our faces. We somehow never ran out of things to talk about, and every conversation felt like progress toward the best selves we were meant to be.

"It never goes away, does it?" he said, referring to our connection, and I sobbed, immediately. He said what I felt: that no matter where I went or what I did, this hopeless love would still be there. He wrapped his arms around me, and I cried on his shoulder. Then we picked ourselves up and went inside.

Adam came into my room to use the bathroom, though we both knew it wasn't really for that, because his room was only a few doors down. I don't know whether he pulled or I pushed, but suddenly I was on top of him, and we were kissing. I think.

It was so surreal, so unexpected, so wanted, that I only remember glimpses, flashes, as in a dream. The characters even changed at times, floating in and out of their bodies, superimposing and replacing one another. Sometimes I wasn't me but this other girl watching from the outside. Sometimes he wasn't him but this other man, a man I didn't know.

I have no memory of how we became naked. Our clothes dissolved and vaporized. There was no sound. I felt as though we were floating in cotton that absorbed our every sense. Every sound, sight, smell, touch, taste—gone into the cotton. Only flashes of memory remain, and those flashes are the stings of disappointment.

Disappointment that his hands fumbled, when in every other way he was smooth and confident.

Disappointment that he laid back, straight-faced and paralyzed, when he normally took the lead.

Disappointment that no matter how I tried, I couldn't make the same meaningful eye contact that we had shared on a daily basis, on occasions far less momentous.

Disappointment, most of all, that he wasn't tender, the way he was when he touched my knee beneath the table or my back when we entered a room together.

I thought he would raise his hand to softly stroke my cheek. I thought he would run his fingers through my hair. I thought he would kiss my forehead, my neck, my shoulder, every square inch of my body, adoring me. I thought he would look me in the eyes and tell me I'm beautiful. I thought he would pull me in and hold me tight like he never wanted to let go. I thought we would make love, because I loved.

"Did you?" he asked, breathing heavily.

"No," I said.

"What do you think that means?"

"It means you have more work to do," I said, forcing a laugh, trying to reclaim what we were in the daylight, to somehow see the faces of the characters within the dream.

He tried. But no touch, no matter how skillful or well placed, could make up for the fact that he did not touch my face.

When the alarm sounded at 5 a.m., we couldn't believe it. He checked his watch, he checked his phone, I checked my phone. More than five hours had passed. We had to be on set in an hour.

We both got up, not saying a word, and we stepped into the shower together as though we'd been doing this all our lives. I washed him, and he washed me, in a mechanical kind of way, with one of those waxy little bars of cheap hotel soap. We dried off sharing a single crunchy towel, and we got dressed.

"I never wanted to be that guy," he said, staring at the wall, his guilt rising with the sun. He was that guy, whether he wanted to be or not, and I was that girl. I didn't want to be *that girl*. I wanted to be *the girl*, his only girl, forever and ever.

After the long day's shoot, the company president decided it was time to go. They were scheduled to stay one more night, but he was ready to get out of the third-world and back to his first-class home.

"Will Erin be okay here on her own?" the vice president asked. They had arrived with full security detail, flashing lights and black suits in tow, and they were about to leave me alone in a country with an exceedingly high homicide rate.

"I'll be fine," I said. I don't know why I said this, because I wanted them to stay one more night. I wanted one more chance for Adam to love me. Within an hour, their flights were changed, and they would leave for the airport shortly.

"Let's get a drink," Adam said, and we went to the hotel bar. The others didn't follow. I suspect they knew this was meant to be a private conversation. The two of us sat in silence, a rarity, and sipped our *cuba libres*.

"We can't tell anyone," he said.

"I told Jen."

"What? Already? Why did you do that?"

"I was excited," I said, being honest, as I always was with him. He took a drink.

"Well, we satisfied our curiosity," he said, as though wrapping up a project. When he said this, I knew I should feel hurt, but I was still numb, uncertain whether I was inside a dream that had turned nightmare.

"It felt really disconnected to me," I told him.

"Really? I didn't feel that way." He ordered us two more drinks.

"I wish you guys weren't leaving."

"Yeah, I don't know why we are. It's stupid."

"The cab's here," the vice president advised.

"Alright chica, I guess we've got to go." He gave me a hug and cradled the back of my head, tender like I knew him before we went and fucked it all up.

A WORK OF ART

W hen I got back to Cusco, I wrote Elías on Facebook.
I wanted to know why he got kicked out of the shelter, and I wanted to make sure he was okay. I always felt a
connection to him, though five years ago my Spanish was so
basic I could hardly understand the stories he told me. We
planned to meet for a coffee in the central Plaza de Armas.

Seeing Elías was like seeing a bright light at the end of a
dark tunnel. He came up behind me, startling me, and I
spun around to give him a big hug. A familiar face, a good
soul.

"Where should we go for coffee?" I asked. "Or a beer." He
was, after all, twenty-four years old now—only four years my
junior.

"Let's get a beer," he said, suggesting the iconic Norton's
bar on the corner by the cathedral.

I soon learned the reason that Elías had been kicked out,
and it made me even more upset with the orphanage for
becoming more of an exclusive club than a shelter.

"I took all the pills," Elías said, his face kind and honest.

"I didn't care what happened to me." In a moment of severe depression, he had swallowed a random mix of pills that landed him in the emergency room. "They said I was a bad influence for the kids, so, I can't live there anymore."

"I think they need you there," I said. "Herbert is so boring. He doesn't play with the kids like you did."

"I don't want to go back. It's better being on my own."

"Where are you living now?"

"In Ttío. I have a room in a lady's house, on the top floor. I pay a little more, but you can see the mountains." ('A little more' meant eighty U.S. dollars per month as opposed to seventy-five.)

"Are you still studying?" When I last saw Elías, a European couple was going to sponsor him to study psychology at the university.

"I dropped out. I don't want to study psychology. I want to do art. But they won't let me do that, because they don't think it can make money. But I know that I can."

"I like your confidence. I remember the painting you did. It was really good."

"My new stuff is different. Would you like to see it?" he asked with pleading eyes.

"Of course I would," I said. We left and hailed a combi headed for the suburb of Ttío, about halfway between the center and my place.

We climbed four flights of stairs, past a growling mangy dog nipping at my heels, to the top terrace. Like all terraces in poor areas of Cusco, it was incomplete, a dense rebar jungle emerging from gray cement blocks. They tell me that no one finishes their construction projects in Peru, because, once you finish, you have to start paying property taxes.

Cuys, guinea pigs that the landlord raised for food, squeaked their peculiar dog-toy sound.

Freshly laundered clothes, smelling of concentrated detergent, fluttered on the line in the cold Andean breeze.

Tripe stewed in the landlord's kitchen and accosted my nostrils.

Elías smiled, showing an attractive gap between his two front teeth. He hunched his shoulders and opened the wooden door into the tiny, cold, concrete room. "No es nada." *It's nothing.*

Panoramic windows in front of us revealed a green blanket of rippled Andean mountains.

"Elías. It's breathtaking."

"It's a disaster," he said, as he worked to organize his things, which my eyes took in with great interest. Paint brushes and paper strewn everywhere. Bracelets he had made from yarn. A twin mattress on the floor in the corner. A single mug and bowl. A bag of rice that accounted for the bulk of his meals. A camera. Piles of hand-me-down clothes, most too big or ripped in places. Books on art, books on love, books on sex, books on psychology, books on top of books on top of books.

"That's my favorite mountain, El Picol," Elías said, pointing to a rounded one. "We can climb it one day."

"I would like that," I said.

He gathered some of the papers from the ground and desk, humble and unhurried. "Do you want to see?"

"Yes." We sat on the floor bed, and he showed me each painting, one by one. The paintings were good, but more impressive were his deep, intellectual explanations of them.

"This is a girl who is caught between two worlds," he explained of an abstract, Dali-inspired painting. "On one side, she is a woman. She has her job, her family, her home, and she takes care of everything. On the other side, she is just a little girl. She is afraid, insecure. She wants to play and be free."

"These are very special, Elías."

"You can have this one," he said, perhaps intuiting that I was that woman-girl.

"You're really talented, you know."

"I'm going to be big one day," he said, and I believed it with him, with every fiber of my being.

The connection I felt to him before was still undeniably there. About my height at five-foot-four, with scoliosis, skinny arms and gapped teeth, Elías was not conventionally attractive, but, to me, he was the most beautiful thing in the world.

Elías's skin was golden. Light shone from the depths of his soul, out through his pores making him glow, and I was not the only one who could see it.

A thirty-four-year-old man from England had tattooed one of Elías's bracelet patterns on his calf and would visit next month. A Swedish, middle-aged woman and her daughters planned to visit him next year. That European couple chose him to sponsor at university, before he dropped out.

He was covered with scars. Cuts on his shins, from dad's military boots. Thick centipede slices into his neck and collarbone, where they took out the cancer at age eleven. A lightning bolt across a bony knee, from a fall on concrete at the shelter.

Despite having nothing, an abused and abandoned boy from the streets, Elías had a long list of international admirers: a blonde from Denmark, a redhead from England, and, now, a brunette from Oregon. I kissed him.

I woke the next morning to him gingerly shutting the door, returning from an outing. He sat beside me on the floor-bed and handed me fresh-squeezed orange juice in a plastic bag with a straw, as they serve it in Peru, and a single red rose. I sat up, eyebrows arched in melting appreciation of this act of kindness that my soul so needed.

If it's any wonder to you why I stayed with him the rest of my time there, you've never had your heart buried alive, doomed to death, and then subsequently shown a tunnel of light back to the land of the living. Elías, despite all his own torments and traumas, was my savior, and I selfishly absorbed his every kindness.

He held me nights as I cried, while he told me over and over, "Sácalo todo, nena." *Get it all out, darling.*

He let me sleep the whole day, staying by my side though he would have liked to be more active. "Do you want to go run?" he would ask. I would curl up into the fetal position without answering, and he would lie back down at my side.

He listened to me go on about another man whom I loved, and he reminded me that I deserve more, someone who is there for me all the time.

He brought me a new journal while I waited for the doctor, with a red-spotted rash from head to toe.

He ran to the market to get eucalyptus leaves and boiled them into a tea when my throat was so sore I couldn't speak.

He tenderly put socks on my feet as I laid in a hospital bed, hooked up to an IV and burning up with fever.

I went to several doctors, but nobody could find what was wrong.

"It's an allergic reaction," said one.

"It's salmonella," said another.

"It's gastroenteritis," said yet another.

Test after test came back negative, and yet I spent hours of every day in the fetal position, stomach twisting, hair falling out, lymph nodes swollen.

Conventional doctors couldn't figure it out, but soon we would meet Ibán the shaman, who knew what they did not. I suffered from "too much feelings," a broken heart that even Peru could not cure.

SOMETHING IMPULSIVE

After nearly three months in Peru, I had to go back to Oregon. I had promised the marketing agency I would return, and my little brother Cory was getting married. I also was still awfully ill and hoped U.S. doctors might help.

As each leg of the trip brought me closer, my dread increased. On the flight from Cusco to Lima, I felt uneasy. From Lima to San Francisco, I felt ill. As I waited on the San Francisco tarmac for our departure to Portland, where Cory's wedding would take place, my stomach twisted and my ego taunted: They're all going to see that you're sad. You're supposed to be happy now. You got what you wanted, didn't you? You have been whining about going to Peru for five years and, look, it didn't make a difference. You failed. You're a failure. You're still sad.

In a little over two hours, my family would pick me up and we'd go to the big rental home where parents, aunts, cousins and soon-to-be in-laws were staying in anticipation of the wedding. Moms in particular have a way of sniffing it out, seeing the sadness in your eyes even when your mouth is smiling and you say all the right things. So, I went in for my methadone. I opened up my flight aggregator app and searched flights to "Everywhere."

Europe, too expensive.
Asia, too far.
Jamaica, too dangerous.

I made a list of the things I wanted in my life:

Warm weather
Beaches
Handsome men
Spanish

Then logic hit me upside the head. I only had two thousand dollars in the bank and still was paying half a mortgage on the Oregon home. (Though the divorce was final, John and I were still amicably sorting that piece out.) I made good money at the marketing agency and, if I left, I had nothing. No job, no home, no plan, no one.

"There's always a way," I recalled a fellow traveler saying one night, as we all sat around chatting in one of the hostels on the way to Machu Picchu. He explained his non-plan. "I don't have much money, but I'll just go up to Cartagena, hang out at the docks and get a job on one of the boats there."

I searched Cartagena, Colombia, one-way.

$296.

That price was unheard of! Departing from small-town Medford, Oregon, exactly two months from today. The plane started rolling, and I was about to lose my signal. With two seats left at that price, I had to make a move. I filled out my passenger details, as I talked myself through it.

I've always wanted to go to Colombia. Everyone says it's beautiful. I can find a job, right? It can't be that expensive. I'll sell my car. Where will I live? The plane rolled down the runway as I typed in my credit card number. It has everything I want, the Caribbean, sunny and warm with coconuts and palm trees. What will my work say? I'll give them two months notice. I need this. If I change my mind, it's only $296. I can't go wrong, really. Yes, let's do this, let's get away, miles away, from Oregon and family and Adam and sadness and heartbreak and failure. As the plane accelerated, I hit "Book It."

Congratulations! You are going to Cartagena!

My heart swelled, and I grasped my palms over my mouth and nose, laughing out loud. There we go. A nice shot of happiness, to fool my friends, my family—and myself— that everything was okay.

I sent Adam one last message before shutting down my phone for the flight.

ERIN

I just did something impulsive.

SOUL WITH ME

As if by miracle, days after I booked my one-way ticket to Colombia, John decided we could sell the house. I was desperate for funds, but I hadn't pushed the issue. He and his wonderful dad had built the house together, so it had sentimental value. But John decided that his recent move to Alaska would be permanent, so I moved into the house, alone, and prepared it for sale.

On a Saturday morning, at 7 a.m., I also prepared to sell everything inside it, all that we had accumulated over eight years of marriage and ten years together. I got my home-made MOVING SALE signs ready and pushed the garage door opener, the motor whirring as it lifted.

"Holy shit," I said, hitting the button again to stop the door from lifting further. There were seven cars parked in the driveway, no doubt full of senior citizens and pawn shoppers ready to devour the remnants of my life. All our things were piled there but not yet priced or organized. Not wanting to lose business, I ran inside, put on a bra and opened the door for the vultures.

"How much is this?" A woman with a front-butt filling her cotton pants held up my black and red coffee maker with the digital clock and six settings.

"Ummm, thirty dollars?"

"Will you take ten," she stated.

"No, it's really worth about sixty. How about twenty?"

"Ten."

Another woman with stringy brown hair and Coke-bottle glasses interrupted. "The ad said there's a couch."

"Oh yeah, it's inside. If you're interested..." Before I could finish, she pushed in the door connecting the garage to the house. "Wait!" I ran after her. The woman with the coffeemaker was busy trying on my shoes.

Coke-Bottles sat on the couch and wiggled side to side. "How much you want for it?"

"I'm selling the whole set for six hundred."

"I just want the couch." She laid down and put her Crocs up on the arm.

"I'm selling the whole set," I repeated.

Front-Butt called from outside. "I'm ready. How much for all this?" She had her arms filled with the coffee maker, my high heels, John's flannels and homemade Christmas decorations.

"Coffee maker twenty bucks, shirts like two dollars each, decorations five dollars altogether, shoes ten dollars, soooo thirty-seven for everything?"

"Twenty." She dangled a crumpled twenty-dollar bill between her sweaty fingers.

I breathed in deep through my nose as two more strangers pushed past me, through the open door into my house. "Okay." I snatched the twenty and ran inside.

Three people were in my off-limits bedroom, one fingering through my jewelry case, another palming my pistol and the third holding up my bedspread. "This stuff isn't for sale!" I didn't mean to yell. Most of my life was, but not this stuff.

"How much for the vanity?" asked a pretty, redheaded woman with a soft voice and crocheted shawl.

"I wasn't planning on selling it." I had just picked it up at an antique shop a week before, for a writing desk.

"It's just what I'm looking for."

"Thirty?"

"Does it come with the stool?"

I breathed in through my nose. "Sure." I dumped the drawers upside-down to empty them onto the floor. In about thirty seconds, her husband had hoisted it onto his shoulder and hauled it out to their truck.

My phone rang. "Erin, it's Steve, your realtor."

"Hey, Steve, what's up? I'm kind of busy. Got the garage sale going on, you know. People are crazy!"

He laughed. "Yes they can be. I have some news for you, though, and I'd like to tell you in person. Will you be in town today?"

"Not before six. Can it wait until Monday?" The house had been on the market just two days, so whatever it was couldn't be that important.

"I live out that way, so I'll stop by on my way home."

"Okay, thanks Steve. Sorry. This is hectic."

Over the next eight hours, people kept coming and I kept saying "sure" until all the things we had so carefully selected and once so desperately wanted were loaded into other peoples' arms and cars, gone to the garage sale vultures forever.

Around 4 p.m., the realtor pulled up and parked at the end of the long line of cars in the driveway.

"Hi, Steve. Can I get you something to drink?"

"No thanks, I'm alright. It looks like your sale is going well."

"Yeah, it's unbelievable. I can't believe how many people are out garage-saleing in January."

"Well, I have some other good news for you."

"Yeah? What's up? Is somebody interested?"

"More than interested. You've received an offer."

My heart fluttered. Soon to be jobless, homeless, planless, I needed this. "How much?"

"The full asking price. They loved it, and they want to move forward right away."

I must have taken a long time to respond, and I don't remember what I said. I felt a confusing combination of divine confirmation and can't-turn-back-now melancholy. Everything John and I had worked for over the past ten years would be gone, really gone.

To get here, we had made so many sacrifices, which I thought were just meatless spaghetti and high-water pants, but what we really lost, to the sixty-hour work weeks and a frugal focus on someday, was us. After the second year of our marriage, we didn't take long drives in the country anymore, because it would use up gas and time. We didn't buy each other gifts, because it would deplete the savings account. We didn't go on dates alone, because it would be a good opportunity to catch up with Dave and Lisa or Matt and Sarah. We didn't do this and we didn't do that. We didn't.

At 6 p.m., I closed the garage door, sat down on the driveway outside, and let my head fall back against the lap siding I had insisted on. I closed my eyes, felt the sun on my face and breathed in deep through my nose, thankful. I felt light and free and unattached to anything or anyone, for the first time in my life.

I heard the crackle of rock under tires but refused to open my eyes.

"Hallo?" Crowed a woman. "Hallo are you still open?"

Do I look open? The garage door and my eyes are closed. I rolled my head forward and forced a straight-lipped smile, then said what I'd said a thousand times that day. "Sure."

I opened the door for one final customer. "Let me know if you need anything!" I yelled back at her as I went inside to drink a beer. I had earned it.

"How much are these books?" She crowed.

"Free!" I yelled back from my spot inside, leaning against the kitchen counter, swigging back apricot ale.

"Free?"

I finished the beer and walked back outside to see the short, Tweedle-Dee-shaped woman in a purple, embroidered moo-moo, stacking books high onto one forearm.

"Sure. Free."

"I have far too many books as it is. My whole floor is just stacks of books."

I laughed. "I understand. I'm going to die surrounded by all the books I meant to read."

"Have you read all of these?" She looked me in the eyes, and I noticed that she had pretty, light-blue eyes that complemented her white feathered hair.

"Most of them. This is my favorite." I pulled C.S. Lewis's *The Weight of Glory* off the shelf, added it to her stack, and recited a quote from memory. "'It would seem that Our Lord finds our desires not too strong, but too weak...We are far too easily pleased.'"

She smiled and nodded knowingly, as though she had heard it or something like it before. "Where are you moving to?"

"Colombia," I said. I had answered this question all day and received all kinds of responses, everything from, "You sellin' cocaine?" to, "You go, girl!"

Her response was unique.

"You have to follow your own knowing," she said.

I smiled. "I'm trying."

"I used to travel, when I was young like you. Sure, everyone thought I was crazy, and now I'm just a lonely old lady with a lot of cats. And books. But I have no regrets for my life. I did everything exactly how I wanted, and there's a lot to be said for that."

I felt a chill, the good kind of chill, move through my spine. "There is a whole lot to be said for that."

"I wrote a haiku, years ago, that I think you'll appreciate," she said, heaving the books back onto the shelf so she could recite it unencumbered.

"In all my travels,
I'm glad my soul went with me,
As such a fine friend."

FLATTERED AND FURIOUS

At 8:42 p.m., I had been at the office nearly twelve hours and had written one hundred words for a press release and more than ten thousand words texting, mostly to Adam. I made myself pack up and head "home," to an empty house and solitude.

When I got there, my phone battery was at eight percent. I dug through my purse for the charger. Unable to feel it with the purse braille that every woman learns, I dumped the contents on the floor of the second bedroom where I was sleeping, since I had rented out the master to a young coworker. Dread seized me as I realized the worst: I left my charger at the office.

I pawed through kitchen drawers and packed boxes, my desperation increasing. Five percent battery. I found intertwined, knotted cords of all shapes and sizes, but that particular little flat-mouthed end I needed for the iPhone was nowhere to be found. I sat on my bed and pouted. What was I going to do here, all alone?

I could drink or call my friend-with-benefits to have

meaningless sex, as I had been doing to numb the pain these days, but those methods hadn't been working out so well, so I took out my journal.

I couldn't think of a thing to write, but I did keep thinking of things to text, so I started documenting my impulses.

> 7:05 Want to tell Adam I always use the fancy new pen he got me for Christmas.
>
> 7:07 Want to ask him for help loading my pen cartridge, though it looks pretty easy.
>
> 7:08 Want to tell him there's a thunderstorm outside. We both love thunder.
>
> 7:09 Want to send him a photo of my messy room. He always said my messiness was endearing.
>
> 7:10 Want to tell him I started reading Tolstoy, like he recommended.
>
> 7:11 Want to tell Jen that this is hard, not talking to him.
>
> 7:14 Want to tell him that I'm sorry for being feisty earlier today.
>
> 7:16 Want to tell him that I miss him.
>
> 7:17 Want to tell him that I'm lonely.
>
> 7:19 Lonely. So lonely I could die.

My eyes watered as it became clear that I was sick, really sick, completely addicted to his attention and affirmation.

As my friend Bri pointed out pre-Peru, moving away wasn't going to fix anything if I didn't fix what was wrong inside of me. I decided, then and there, that the day I left for Colombia, I would quit all "immediate media," all communication methods where I could quickly and easily contact him:

No more texting.

No more email.

No more Facebook.

No more Twitter.

No more Instagram.

No more Words With Friends.

No more Skype.

Without immediate media, our entire relationship wouldn't have progressed. We wouldn't have been able to spend the kind of time together that texting enabled with its direct intravenous line into one another's lives.

He could talk to me while I watched *The Bachelorette* on my mom's couch. Talk to me while I sat in the living room with my husband. Talk to me while I sipped coffee in a Cusco café. Talk to me while I laid in bed nights with insomnia. Talk to me morning, day and night without ever having to look me in the eyes and consider the power of those words and how they might implode my entire life (which, granted, I also took part in imploding).

Adam had pitched me tens of thousands of insincere words that broke my heart, and I was done playing catch. Every single way that he and I had communicated for the past year—every way he made me smile and laugh and love and pine and cry—would be gone.

With my phone dead and no escape, I faced the page and wrote:

January 8, 2014
Soon, I will disconnect from the one form of communication I have with him. Why would I deny myself this great gift, someone who truly understands me and

cares to listen? Because I know that the gift isn't really mine.

He is like a favorite library book that you have to return, after all. As much as you want to reference it and read it over and over, thumb through its pages in the comfort of your bedroom, you have to give it up and give it back to the library at the end of the day.

I would try to remember my favorite lines and phrases, to carry me through to our next meeting, but it wasn't as clear or beautiful as the real thing.

So, knowing it was wrong, but loving that library book with all my soul, I tried to steal it. I wanted it to be mine and only mine, all hours of the day and night. But I couldn't, because it didn't want to be stolen. It liked where it sat, comfortable and familiar, though misunderstood and misfiled.

Was I foolish? To not go to the library because the book couldn't be mine forever? Couldn't I keep checking it out, memorizing what it holds so I could carry its wisdom with me in my mind and heart? Why did I need so badly to possess it?

I tried to find others like it at the bookstore, but they all bored me. And they didn't speak to me the way this particular library book did.

So I stopped going to the library, stopped reading it, gave up my library card, because it was all I wanted to do. I knew that I could never find a new book, one that was completely mine, if I didn't cut myself off from the library book forever. Would I ever find so good a book in all my life?

I kept on writing, there on my bed in the quiet room, with no text notifications or Facebook message bells or work calls ringing in. I wrote five then ten pages without thinking and, then, it got hard. I started looking around frantically for my iPhone—a procrastination parry—but, remembering it was dead, I turned back to the page.

The words started flowing again, and I had completed forty-four handwritten pages before I finally laid down the pen and decided to rest. I was crying, once again, but it was different. My whole body tingled, and I felt something I hadn't felt in a long time, something I didn't know I had been missing. I felt purpose.

As good as the previous night felt without my phone, as soon as I got to the office the next morning, I plugged in and checked my messages. I smiled at the thick stack-up from Adam then told him about my plan, hoping that, when threatened with losing me not only in the physical but the virtual realm, he would finally turn all those empty words into actions.

On January 9, 2014

ADAM

I think I'm sensitive. I'm really sad.

ERIN

You are?

ADAM

How can I not be?

ERIN

I understand.

ADAM

My best friend is moving away and going off the grid.

I'm happy and excited, but sad.

It's the definition of melancholy.

ERIN

It's hard to be your best friend, Adam.

ADAM

I'm sorry.

ERIN

I can't talk to you face-to-face. I can't spend time with you, I can only sometimes reach you. You're worth it, but it's hard.

ADAM

I know. I feel the same way.

You're worth it.

That's why I do it.

But I never want to make your life hard.

I should be adding joy to your life.

If I'm not doing that, it's unhealthy for you.

ERIN

I can't talk about this right now, at work. It's too much. I'll tag back in later.

ADAM

Okay. I understand.

Sometimes I would try to ignore his messages, but then he would send a work-related message that he knew I'd have to respond to. I'd answer then fall right back in, like Alice down the rabbit hole.

On January 21, 2014

ADAM

Hey, where are you?

ERIN

I'm here. Just beginning this media weaning process. :)

ADAM

Ohhh. I get it. :) Please don't wean too hard. This is about the only way I get to talk to you.

On January 22, 2014

ERIN

I'm really sorry. I just need to stop needing you. So I was working on that. Trying. Guess I'm not very good at it.

ADAM

I understand. I do. It doesn't feel good, though.

I don't like it.

ERIN

I don't either. It doesn't feel good for me either. But it also doesn't feel good when I need you and you're not there.

You say you're always here for me...but the fact is that you're just not and you can't be and I understand but it hurts.

ADAM

:(

I keep reading this, keep thinking of something to say, but I can't think of anything.

I want this time to be a celebration.

And I want to be a part of it.

Everyone gets to be a part of it but me.

And, well, that sucks.

We have very little time before you go. I want us to be able to enjoy it and share it with each other.

ERIN

We can't.

It is what it is.

I quoted that particular phrase, "It is what it is," as punishment. He had used it to describe our situation, and I loathed that dry philosophical approach to our destined love. He sent fifteen more texts before I begged him:

ERIN

Please stop.

ADAM
:(Okay.

I sat on the couch and pulled my knees up to my chest. My face turned ugly with sadness, my mouth a clamshell and my forehead an accordion. The outside corners of my eyes filled until the tears dripped down my temples and into my ears. I held the phone facedown against my chest and cried.

Throughout that final month, Adam texted me a lot of emotions, including a few "I love yous" and the proclamation that he would never stop missing me. But the words felt hollow so long as they didn't lead to him choosing me. Maybe he did love me, and maybe he would miss me, but he didn't choose me. And that's why I had to go.

Days before I left for Colombia, Adam sent me a picture of his new, private P.O. box so I could write to him while I was disconnected. I was flattered, and furious.

18

THE DISCONNECT

As I rode to the airport in the early morning darkness, I contemplated the new life I would begin in fewer than twenty-four hours. I started texting my final goodbyes, knowing this was my last chance to blast out some media before my experiment in social solitude began.

I posted one last message to my Facebook timeline:

On February 03, 2014
Dear friends,
I'm going off-grid for a while, going back to basics. If you need to reach me, contact my mom on Facebook, and she'll pass on my mailing address for wherever I am at the time. First stop: Colombia. Much love. xoxo.

I was tempted to look at the likes, all the messages on Facebook congratulating me for quitting, but I decided it negated what I was trying to do and stayed strong.

One by one, I deleted all of my communication apps:

Facebook. Delete.
WhatsApp. Delete.
Instagram. Delete.
Twitter. Delete.
Skype. Delete.
Words With Friends. Delete.
Gmail. Delete.

Once I landed in Colombia, my U.S. SIM card wouldn't work anymore, so that would stop the endless barrage of text messages. iPhone Messages wouldn't let me delete it, so I turned off push notifications and moved it to the third page of my phone where any red message bubbles wouldn't be seen.

At the ticket counter, I handed my passport to the ticket agent, proud of how skilled I'd become at traveling both frugally and fluidly.

"How many bags?"

"Just two."

"That'll be seventy dollars."

"What?"

"Seventy dollars for a second bag."

"Ohhh, no," I smiled at her incompetence. "I'm traveling internationally."

"Right." She didn't smile. "Seventy."

"Since when did you start charging for a second bag?" I reached for my phone like a reflex but stopped myself. I was no longer allowed to message my every trial and triumph to Adam.

"Since January," she said, looking past my upset face to the growing line behind me. I pulled out my credit card and my phone. I began to text him but backspaced.

JEN

Erin are you there? Oh my God, you won't believe it, Brian wrote me just now and said, 'whats up.' What should I say? What does this mean?

I took a deep breath and rubbed the side of my neck. It was so hard to disconnect. The world didn't want me to. It kept forcing its way into my world with push notifications, like a warm slime oozing over my body.

ADAM

Goodbye Erin. I miss you.

With that, I started spilling it all, like a drug addict, itching for one last fix.

ERIN

I miss you too, Adam.

You won't believe what they're talking about behind me.

Havana. Of all places. They're talking about how it's the most romantic city in the world.

Before I left, Adam and I had made a pact to meet one another in Havana in five years, on a particular date that was special to us. I stared at the screen. He hadn't yet responded, but I couldn't stop myself from text-bombing him with every thought inside my head, as we had both been doing for months now.

ERIN

And you won't believe it; they're charging for a second bag on international flights now.

> Ugh, the bathroom here is so gross.

> Made it through security.

Where was he? This was his last chance to talk to me before I disappeared, and he didn't even care. I felt like crying. No, I was crying. I felt so alone, and I looked to my left and right to see if the other passengers could see my loneliness. They were on their phones.

ADAM

Sorry, I was in a meeting.

I wiped my eye with the back of my hand.

ERIN

Your favorite.

ADAM

Oh yeah. #KillMe

ERIN

I'm about to board.

ADAM

This is really it.

ERIN

Sigh. #melancholy.

ADAM

You'll do great. Write that book. Live the dream.

And one more thing...

ERIN

Yes?

ADAM

Something I need to tell you.

ERIN

Tell me.

ADAM

Something you need to know.

This is it. I held my breath. He is finally going to choose me and he's about to say it, now that he sees what he's about to lose. I watched the ellipsis. The PA system warbled, "Boarding zone three. All passengers seated in zone three please make your way to the boarding gate."

ERIN

What is it?

ADAM

I'm proud of you.

I turned off my phone and filed toward the gate with a somber face, my self-inflicted excommunication feeling like an execution.

19

#OCEANVIEW

As we descended into Cartagena, it was clear how messed up I really was. I was about to land in one of the most beautiful cities in the world, a UNESCO world heritage site, and I didn't envision my toes in the sand, the breeze in my hair, the warm salty ocean or cool coconut water, the vibrant Caribbean colors, personalities and percussions. I didn't think of any of that.

I imagined what I would text Adam. I imagined an Instagram filter of Cartagena, a 140-character version, a status update, a quip, a bite, a piece, all of which I would learn were too small to capture the reality I was about to encounter.

A taxi took me to the apartment I'd reserved in Laguito, an upscale district on the tip of the peninsula, with the Caribbean Sea on one side and the Bay of Cartagena on the other.

The taxi driver knew the building immediately by its name, and, when we pulled up to the ivory-colored steps spanning the wide majestic entrance, I understood why. I looked up at the white, fifteen-story building, amazed that I would be living in this luxurious place for 650,000 Colombian pesos a month, about 333 U.S. dollars at the time. This was not the freezing concrete room of Cusco.

The driver helped me lug my bloated bags up the steps, where I entered a sparkling, white-tiled reception area with palm-patterned couches and a big mahogany check-in desk, with mailbox cubbies covering the back wall.

"Hola, buenos días," I said, greeting the smiling Afro-Colombian man in a white, short-sleeved button-up.

"Buenos días. ¿En qué te puedo servir?" *Good morning. How may I serve you?*

"Estoy aquí para visitar a Benicio." *I'm here to visit Benicio.*

"Ahora lo llamo." *I'll call him now*, he said, picking up the phone and dialing my host, whom I found on AirBnb and only "knew" via virtual chat. The receptionist listened and nodded to the phone. "Have a seat. They will come for you soon."

I plopped on the couch, grinning from the inside out. After twenty minutes of waiting, I wondered if maybe I had made a mistake. This was too good to be true. Maybe my building was actually the dilapidated one with exposed rebar that we passed by the airport on the outskirts of town.

"Miss," the man said. "They are ready for you. You can go up now."

I rode the mirrored elevator to the fourth floor and knocked. I knocked again. And again.

The door flew open and a skinny girl in a cotton spaghetti-strapped night gown passed in a flash and disappeared. I stepped into the kitchen, leaving my things in the hallway.

"Perdón," a voice said. *Excuse me.* I scanned the long

narrow apartment, looking for where the voice had come from. She bust out of swinging saloon-style doors to my right with a broom and swept around my feet as she spoke fast Spanish. "It's a mess. We had a guest in your room and we're getting it cleaned up now." She stopped for a moment and looked me in the eyes. "I'm Mia."

Mia was about five-foot tall and no more than ninety pounds. She had long, thick black hair with a bright yellow-blonde layer on top that flopped into her eyes. Mia was fast. She talked fast, swept fast, thought fast. Within minutes, I knew not only where my room was but that Mia was a twenty-year-old communist, vegetarian, Capoeira enthusiast who had been diagnosed with ADHD, had a boyfriend she met on Facebook, and that Mia was going to get a boob job but didn't think a butt job was necessary because she could build it up with exercise. Mia was crazy, passionate and full of ideas. I liked Mia.

I set my things in my spacious room, which looked just like the pictures, with white tile floors, dark wood closets spanning an entire wall, a twin bed and a window over-looking the bay.

"Benicio will be home soon," Mia said. "He's bringing your sheets. Do you like to cook? I love to cook. Here, try this." She poured me a tall glass of off-white liquid. "It's homemade soy milk."

"Mmm, it's good. How do you make it?"

She crawled on the counter and pulled down soy beans from the top shelf and started to show me.

"Do you have a boyfriend?" she asked. In Latin American culture, this was a common first line of questioning.

"No, no boyfriend."

"That's okay. You're young. Do you work out?"

"I used to. I need to again."

"I go to a really good gym. You can come with me if you want. I want to be a *garota*."

"What's a garota?"

She speed-walked to the computer in the living room and pulled up Google images of nearly naked Latina women wearing sequined bras, G-strings and feather headdresses that they displayed at Colombian Carnaval. I nodded. "Pretty."

"I'm a biology major. I didn't do well in school, but I'm smart. They say I have ADHD and autism but it's bullshit. The school system just didn't know how to handle my kind of energy."

"I can see that," I said. Her energy was awesome but overwhelming. I wondered, living with her, just how relaxing my Caribbean escape would be.

"I've got to teach you some things," she said, walking into her bedroom and expecting me to follow. "Here, between friends, everyone's *maricas*."

Marica meant gay, as far as I knew. "Maricas?"

"There's no harm meant by it. It's just what we call each other."

She carried a gray tabby cat out of the second bedroom that she, Benicio and their mom would be sharing while I stayed in the guest room.

"This is Josefa," she said. I reached to pet her, and Josefa grabbed onto my hand and bit it hard. "Don't pet her," Mia said. "I rescued her from a gutter and got her all cleaned up. She only likes me." The cat snuggled contentedly against her chest and glared at me.

"Not a problem," I said. (I prefer dogs.)

I followed her back into the living room where she dumped Devil Cat on the couch.

"This is DeeDee." She pointed to a sad white poodle with brown goo around her eyes and pink bows on her ears. "She's old." Devil Cat swatted at DeeDee's face, and DeeDee nipped and growled.

Benicio walked in through the open door carrying stacks of sheets. "Erin!" Beni was a calming presence among the storm that was Mia, Devil Cat and DeeDee. He looked like a mini, pudgy Ricky Martin with his handsome face, stylish floppy hair and tender brown eyes. He was also the only one in the house who spoke English, which I welcomed after getting a taste of the fast and slurred *costeño* Spanish.

"Benicio! It's so good to meet you!"

"You too! I am sorry it is taking me so long to arrive here. I have the sheets for you."

"Okay, thank you. I'll put them on the bed." As he transferred the sheets to my arms, we made eye contact, and I knew we were going to be friends. I went to my room and shut the door to decompress.

Where the old me would start Instagramming and Facebooking photos of my #CaribbeanBrightBedroom with the #OceanView, texting Adam and Jen pictures bragging about my sweet new space, I instead threw on a coral-colored jersey dress over a turquoise bikini and got ready to walk to the historic city center.

When I came out, the mom Dolores had arrived. She looked at me and smiled, but she made me nervous, with her conservative, delicate appearance and prim red lips pressed together. "Hola," she said, leaning in for the customary Colombian hug and kiss on the cheek. She went straight to their bedroom, and I got the impression that this rental idea had not been hers.

"Is it safe to walk alone?" I asked my new house siblings.

"Oh yeah, it's safe all the time," Beni said.

"Is it too far to walk to the center?"

"No, not at all," said Mia. "I always walk."

"Take the beach," said Dolores, peeking out from her room, smiling at me. "It's prettier, and you can follow it all the way there."

"Thank you." I smiled back. She was going to accept me.

"And make sure you put on sunscreen," she said. "Do you need some?"

"Oh, no, I'll be fine. I don't burn," I said, knowing that my Native American skin served me well in sunny climates. Dolores and Mia looked at one another, smirking.

"But you are a gringa. You are so white," Mia said. "You will definitely burn."

I never thought of myself as white, being an olive-skinned person living among a pale-skinned population, but here, I was white. Travel taught me that how you define yourself is largely determined by whom you have around to compare yourself to. I always thought I had dark skin, dark hair, brown eyes. Here, they told me I had light skin, blonde hair and green eyes (which I still can't see, but I heard it multiple times).

Sans sunscreen, per my stubborn refusal, I walked the one block to the beach and kicked off my flip-flops as soon as the ground underfoot melted from sidewalk to sand. After twenty-four hours of flights and layovers, my hair was greasy and my eyes were puffy, with eyeliner smudged beneath from sporadic crying breakdowns. It didn't matter. I had covered the evidence of my instability with sunglasses and couldn't wait to get my toes in the sand and walk alone, for the first time in my life truly alone, without a phone or media popping in to interrupt my peace. I looked around. The air was warm and humid, smelling of fried fresh fish, coconuts, salt and sun tanning oil. A fast-paced percussive reggae music played and people sat on rickety, paint-chipped stools laughing and drinking at thatched roof huts with big yellow banners announcing the national beer, *ÁGUILA.*

The brown-tinged turquoise water spread out before me, full of tourists of all colors and nations who were boogie boarding, kite surfing, jet skiing and jumping up and down like little bobbers in the lolling waves. I walked toward the water, wanting to be part of the beautiful tapestry before me.

"Nena. Nena." *Baby. Baby.* A robust Afro-Colombian woman in tight, knee-length jean shorts squeezing her like a tube of biscuits came waddling toward me fast. "¿Quieres una limonada de coco, muñeca?" *You want a coconut lemonade, doll?*

"¿Cuánto vale?" I asked. *How much is it?*

"Diez mil pesitos." *Just ten thousand lil' pesos.* Pesos became pesitos when they wanted it to sound like no big deal. At that time, the exchange rate was about two thousand Colombian pesos to one dollar, so the gal wanted five dollars.

"¡Diez mil!" I started the haggling game essential to surviving the standard practice of price-gouging gringos. "I'll give you eight thousand."

A balding, stalky man in a striped polo pulled out a rusty machete and hacked the top of the green coconut to pass to Biscuit Shorts. She mixed up the concoction in a plastic pitcher, which she poured into the coconut and topped off with a turquoise straw and a cherry between two orange slices. They took some cheesy pictures of me with my offline phone—holding the coconut, drinking out of the coconut, pointing to the coconut sign and all other variations of coconut craziness, and I was on my way.

I yearned to share it all with Adam, somehow. He would love the juxtaposition of the casual, Caribbean beach with the elegant Spanish cathedrals in the distance, marking the entrance to the historic center. He would dig his toes in the sand with me and find a spot to sit and write for hours, until the sunset came and we grabbed beers at one of the huts and talked about writing and living and all the people we'd seen that day. He would do all of those things—if he loved me, that is.

It was at that moment that I lifted my sunglasses onto my head. Without looking or trying, my eyes connected with the brown, almond-shaped eyes of a handsome, dark-skinned lifeguard about ten feet in front of me. As I passed, he smiled a grand white smile between dark taupe, sensual lips.

I was determined to be alone, to continue on my independent way, so I kept on walking. But I stopped, for only a second, to look back. So did he.

"Hola," he said.

"Hola," I said.

"¿Quieres hablar conmigo?" he asked. *Would you like to talk with me?* He flashed that big white smile. I could be independent later.

We ended up talking for hours, dragging our toes in varying patterns in the sand, touching on everything from past relationships to existentialism to life philosophies. I learned that he was working as a lifeguard for now but would soon graduate with a degree in law. Juan Calderón the

Lifeguard-Lawyer: the muscles and tan of a lifeguard, the mind and tenacity of a lawyer. God help me.

We sat down on the sand as the sun began to drop toward the horizon. I put my legs straight out in front of me, then crossed them, then pulled them into my chest, trying to find the position that made my self-denounced chubby legs look thinner and more attractive. I sucked in my stomach and pulled out the material of my jersey dress to hide a belly from pounds put on over the holidays. He was so handsome, and I felt insecure, fat, pale and American among the stunning Colombian women who all looked like some variation of Sofia Vergara. But all he looked at were my eyes, his own eyes so dark brown that I couldn't distinguish between pupil and iris in the bright sun.

"Do you have a girlfriend?" I asked. Apparently I had embraced the Latin American way.

He paused and waggled his head from side to side. "Tengo...amigas." *I have...friends.*

"So you have a girlfriend, then."

He laughed. "No. Amigas."

That meant he either slept around, a lot, or he had a girlfriend.

"What about you?" he asked. "Do you have a boyfriend?"

"Nope," I said, happy to be untethered.

"Have you ever felt a connection like this before?" he asked.

"No," I said, telling two lies at once. The first lie was that I had never felt this kind of connection before, and the second lie was the implication that I felt it now.

"I never have," he said. He looked into my eyes with his intense, black-coffee eyes and leaned toward me, then stopped himself and sat up straight, looking around and shaking his head. He laughed as he ran his hand over the top of his short, curly black hair. He wanted to kiss me but couldn't while on duty.

"What are you doing tonight? Would you like to go out? I can show you the city," he offered.

"I would love to." I paused and thought of the many times I had forsaken my girlfriends for some pretense of romance, and I checked myself. "But, I already promised my roommate Mia we'd cook dinner together tonight." He nodded, understanding but looking bummed.

"But hey! If I go back there right now, and things have changed, I'll meet you back here at your tower. You said you get off at six, right?"

He grinned. "Vale. Todo bien." *Alright. All good.*

I walked, half ran, back to the apartment, making peace with the fact that I would likely be spending my evening cooking lentils with Mia rather than in the strong arms of Juan Calderón. We hadn't exchanged contact info, because, now that I was off media, I had no phone number, Facebook or WhatsApp to give.

When I got to the apartment, I rode the elevator up the four floors and pushed the handle down to get a KACHUNK. The door was locked. No one was home. I couldn't call Mia, because she, like me, had no cell phone. I unlocked the door, pushed my way inside and did a quick happy dance with DeeDee the poodle before I went careening into my bedroom to get ready.

Rushing though I was, by the time I got back to the beach it was already ten past six. I jogged toward Juan's tower, but at 6:20 I was only halfway there. He was going to think I wasn't coming. I slowed to a walk and resigned myself to the fact that he was gone. Maybe I could saunter by and try to catch his attention another day.

But in the distance, standing at the tower one hundred feet ahead, I saw the bright red shorts and beacon of a white smile. He had waited. I slowed my walk to appear casual and tried to control my ragged, out-of-shape breathing. Juan walked down the ramp and, as soon as I got close enough, he wrapped his arm around my lower back and dipped me back to kiss me.

"Mmmmfh." I didn't know whether to push him away for his presumption or melt into him because I wanted to. I came back up for air. "Hola."

"Hola." He smiled, laughing a little. "Espera aquí." *Wait here.* He walked behind the tower to talk with a knobby-kneed man for a minute and soon returned carrying a white plastic chair on each forearm.

"Come on," he said, grabbing me by the hand. He set the chairs down at the sea's edge and gestured for me to sit. Knobby Knees brought us two beers, and already it felt like the best date of my life.

Juan wanted to know everything, about Oregon, my family, my job, my writing. He wanted to know so much that I was skeptical. He was too good at this. No other man, besides Adam, had ever taken an interest in me like this. And he was interesting. He quoted Freud and Hegel and Nietsche and talked with his hands, which he rested a bit too high on my bare thigh while he listened to me talk about my passions.

I looked down at his hand there and told myself that I would not, should not, sleep with him. I had learned, in my short time in Single-Girl World, that men knew how to be interested and engaging until they got sex, and then they turned a cold shoulder.

No, I would not sleep with him. He adjusted his cap over his black curly hair, and I admired his thick Spanish eyebrows. No, I would not sleep with him for a whole month. I watched his taupe lips explain the legal terms "dolobuenos" and "dolomalos." *Good hurts and bad hurts.* But no. I would not become another of his "amigas." I listened to his deep, raspy voice, his infectious, machine-gun laugh. That's right, I declared to myself. I would not sleep with him for two weeks.

"You want to go see the center now?"

"I really do."

We walked, holding hands, to the center that I had attempted to reach over eight hours ago.

I was glad I waited. Everything was so romantic at night, with soft yellow uplighting on the colonial curves of the cathedrals, with couples click-clacking in their heels and dress shoes on the cobblestone. I wanted to capture all of it. And then put Instagram filters on it and push it out to the world. #Cartagena #LifeguardLawyer #EnvyMe.

"I'll take your picture," Juan said.

"Oh, no, it's okay," I said, wanting pictures but feeling shy.

"Come on."

"Okay, but together." We took a couple of selfies, one facing forward smiling and another with me kissing him on his warm, caramel-colored cheek.

"Now you, in front of the clock tower," he said.

"Okay." I walked over to stand in front of the yellow spire and did the usual girl pose, the one that makes you look as skinny as possible, with one knee bent and a hand on the hip.

"Pose," he directed.

I laughed, feeling awkward, and did the same safe pose again.

"Pose! Another pose." He was playing photographer, turning the camera.

I leaned against a short stout palm tree and extended one arm above my head.

"There you go! Another!"

I faced forward again, bent both knees and blew a kiss. Now I was laughing because this was fun. He laughed, too, and handed me the camera. "Eres hermosa," he said. *You're beautiful.*

One hour later, I was crying.

We had been sitting and talking on a stone bench behind the clock tower, one tree over from where the prostitutes sit fanning themselves and tugging at their tops all night.

Juan leaned in and whispered in my ear. "You want to go somewhere, just you and me?"

"No." I glared at him, shoulders squared in a fighting stance. I felt hurt, disappointed that I was right. I wasn't beautiful. I wasn't special. He didn't feel connected to me. He just wanted to have sex with me and roll over and steal my iPhone. I started to cry.

"What's wrong?" Juan asked. "Is it something I did?"

I choked back tears as I processed my emotions. I wasn't really upset with him for wanting to sleep with me. I was upset with *me* for wanting to sleep with *him*. I had been without media and Adam for fewer than twenty-four hours, and I was already trying to replace one source of affirmation with another. I was completely incapable of living my life without someone to tell me who I was and what I was worth.

"Juan, I like you. But I came here to be alone, so I need to be alone, independent for a while."

"Okay." He looked down and put his hand on my knee. "But Erin, you can be independent and be with someone. There are always going to be people in our lives who help us along the way. Being with someone, enjoying their company, doesn't mean you're not independent."

"You're right," I said, because he was. But I also knew that, recently divorced and subsequently dumped, insecure and clueless as to how to value myself without likes and texts and compliments from a handsome Latin lover, I was not strong enough to know the difference.

Juan walked me to the street and hailed a cab. He gave me a hug. "Eres dulce," he said. *You're sweet.*

"No, you're sweet." I rested my head on his chest.

"You still want to run tomorrow?" Earlier in the evening, we had talked about meeting the next morning to work out together on the beach.

I thought about what he said, about independence. I thought of my brief time living alone in my Oregon country house, building fires, assembling my bed, loading my pistol, airing up tires, carrying heavy shit, doing all the right actions to make me feel empowered, but, at the end of the day, still checking my texts and crying in bed like a baby when Adam hadn't written. Maybe, I thought, independence is not so much about what you do, but what you feel.

"Yeah, I do." I smiled and ducked into the cab, holding my hand up close to the tinted window to wave goodbye.

20

CROSSING THE DISTANCE

"*A*lguna carta para 402B?" *Any letter for 402B?* I asked the front desk the same question I would ask every day for months to come, as I eyed the mahogany cubbies on the wall behind. I had only arrived yesterday, but I thought I'd check, just in case.

I walked ten minutes to Castillogrande, the beach where Juan Calderón and I had agreed to meet. Hardly anyone was there, but I faced away from the ocean, toward the lifeguard tower, to make sure I didn't miss him. One had to be far more punctual and attentive without the aid of a cell phone.

I had dressed as cute as I could for working out, with a pink racerback top and a white tennis skort, my hair in a ponytail with a bump. I pulled the bottom of the tight shirt down and adjusted the spandex shorts of my skort. I sucked in. I checked the clock. 8:01 a.m. That's it. He isn't coming. He's decided that since I'm not easy, he's not interested. Before my mind could spin further out of control with insecurity scenarios, Juan appeared from behind the lifeguard tower, looking even more handsome than the day before.

"¿Estás lista?" *Are you ready?* He pulled down his board shorts to reveal a pair of tight, shiny gray boxer-briefs that my friends would later dub his "hot pants." He was caramel-colored and thin, muscular, about six-foot tall. I was pale from the Oregon winter and twenty pounds overweight.

"Si, lista." *Yes, ready.* We took off running down the beach. Within minutes, my face was flushed and I was breathing heavily.

"Breathe with rhythm," he said, "Like this." He breathed in through his nose and back out through his mouth.

"I've never been good at picking up physical technique," I warned.

"Breathe with me." He grabbed my hand as we ran, and we breathed together. In, out. In, out. It was making sense. It was feeling easier. We ran the length of the beach several times.

"How come you're not sweating?" he asked.

"I never sweat," I said, as though it were something to be proud of. The truth was that I never sweated because I never pushed myself.

"We need to make you sweat," he said. "We're going to sprint." He took off. My sprint was a fast jog at best. He turned around and ran backwards, beckoning with both hands. "¡Vamos!" *Let's go!* I stumbled after him like a kid after donuts. This is humiliating. Why did I agree to this? Oh yeah, because he's gorgeous and dreamy and those hot pants...

"Okay, good job." He walked and I staggered to the shade of the trees beside the tower. I went to sit down. "Not yet." He stopped me. "Now jumping jacks." He started jumping and counting. "One, two, three—ONE. One, two, three—TWO. One, two, three—THREE..."

"How come each one is actually four?" I asked.

He laughed. "That's how we count them. Come on, just to ten."

"Which is actually forty."

"Now I lost count. One, two, three—ONE. One, two, three—TWO..."

When we finally reached ten that was more like eighty, I was ready to collapse. I had begun to break a sweat and my face was red. I wondered if he was molding me, if maybe he thought I had a pretty face but was too fat for someone so fit and handsome to date.

"You want an *arepa*?" He reached into his shoulder-sling bag and pulled out two of the traditional Colombian snacks, deep-fried corn cakes filled with fried egg and meat. This guy obviously didn't care if I was skinny.

"Sure." We sat there under the trees, facing the beach and eating our fried treats.

"Did you do your writing?" I asked. I didn't expect him to show up that morning, and I also didn't expect him to complete the homework we discussed yesterday, one page of writing in English so he could practice. (We always spoke Spanish to one another.)

"I did." He pulled it out of his pocket. "My English is so bad."

"No, I'm sure it's good." I read it and tried to control my expressive face. It wasn't bad; it was horrendous. "Do you have a pen?"

"Here." He pulled one from his bag.

I went through marking errors and explaining them to him. "This should be 'they were' instead of 'they was.' Where you say 'I thing,' you actually mean to say, 'I think.'"

"Aghh." He covered his face with his hand. "I told you I

am really terrible." I cringed at his awkward English accent. He sounded much sexier in Spanish. I tried to be encouraging, but I wondered if I could actually date someone with so little understanding of the thing I loved most.

"Okay, my turn," he said, smiling. Yeah, I could sacrifice English for a smile like that. I handed him my two pages, handwritten in Spanish, and he knit his thick brows in concentration.

On February 5, 2014 [translated from Spanish]
It was a real paradise.

I walked, sometimes ran, through the streets smiling, sometimes laughing.

My makeup was a smile, my moisturizer sunblock, my facewash the saltwater, my exfoliant the sand.

It had everything, Cartagena. Perfect weather, a fresh breeze, only a little cold at night.

No bothersome insects, except for the tiny ants that congregated beneath the trees.

Relaxing water, calm but alive, without sharks or manta rays thanks to the subterranean Spanish wall.

A handsome lifeguard with a big smile and thick Spanish eyebrows, who kissed softly and knew how to talk philosophy.

Friends on every corner, ready to help, to share, to call you "my love," "my life," "my princess."

Yes, it had everything, Cartagena. Every desired thing.

Only one thing was missing, that I wished with all my heart were there, one little thing that I was trying to find. Cartagena had everything, but the only thing missing was me.

I was millions of miles away, and I didn't know how to cross the distance.

"You feel like this?" he asked.

"I do," I said, not explaining why.

"I like how you write," he said. "It's like literature." He marked one thing with the pen and handed it back to me.

"That's all?" I was used to Adam's edits, a beautiful red bloodshed with edits on form and awkwardness and adverbs and clichés.

"It's really good. Your Spanish is so good," he said. I smiled, outside gracious but inside a petulant pouting punk.

"You want to go swimming?" Juan asked. It was hot, and I did, but I certainly wasn't ready for Mr. Lifeguard-Lawyer to see me in a swimsuit.

"Sure." Time to get over myself and get on with living.

I changed in the lifeguard tower, boosting my boobs in my turquoise bandeau top, placing the gold hoops of my bottoms in the exact place on my hips that made me look thinnest. I pinched the layer of fat encapsulating my waist. Oh well, here we go. I opened the door and he was waiting right out front, at the bottom of the wooden ramp.

"Beautiful," he said, in awkward English.

I smiled and laughed, not believing him. "Thanks."

We waded into the bath-warm water, and he hugged me close. I wrapped around him like a koala around a tree, and we kissed.

"You kiss really fast," he said. "Slow down."

"You don't like how I kiss?" I was insulted, but I also knew he was right. I tried to do everything fast. Walk fast, talk fast, rest fast, meditate fast. Let's get this over with already!

I slowed my tongue, and he ran his hands all over my body, down to my ass which he squeezed. He tried to slip a finger into my bikini bottoms, but I grabbed his wrist hard and pushed it away. Nonplussed, he wrapped the rejected hand around my waist, and we kissed and kissed, longer and slower than I had ever let anyone kiss me before.

"Let's swim," he said.

"I'm not very good at swimming," I said. Mom and Dad had me in swimming lessons since I was four, but it always felt more like drowning.

"Show me," he said. I swam a few strokes and came up choking on salt water.

"That's pretty good. You understand the technique."

"Yeah, but I always swallow a ton of water."

"This is the trick. Everyone tries to hold their breath as long as possible, until they're dying for air and come up gasping. Instead, you'll exhaust yourself less if you take a breath with every stroke, like this." He swam one hundred feet out and back like a fish.

I tried his technique, and it was a lot simpler. I swam ten strokes and came up smiling.

"There you go, you got it," he said, rewarding me by pulling me in and kissing me some more.

"You're a good teacher," I said. "I never learn physical techniques quickly, but the way you describe things makes it simple."

After swimming lessons, we sunbathed and talked, while I hoped for him to ask me out again that night. When he didn't, my mind went wild. Why wouldn't he ask me out? Is it because I didn't put out? Didn't we have fun? He must have a girlfriend. He must think I'm fat, now that he saw me wear a bikini at my winter weight.

I had feared that Juan would take away my independence when, really, I was the one doing it. He was content to see me for a little while in the mornings then go about his full life with his law studies and friends. He was giving me space, and I was trying to bridge it. I was taking away my own independence. I was the one.

21

A GLIMPSE OF GOD

That afternoon, I strolled through Cartagena's historic center alone, getting lost in the labyrinth of colonial buildings and balconies covered in bougainvillea.

I took pictures, but not of the same things I used to. I couldn't upload them anywhere or send them to anyone, so they took on a new purpose. They were no longer meant to incite envy over how much fun I was having but were rather a symbol, a snapshot of a time and place where I felt joy and peace.

I photographed bookstores that Adam would wander through and sneakers that Adam would wear and street food that Adam would eat and museums that Adam would visit and pigeons that Adam would call flying rats. There were twinges of him everywhere, it seemed, and I talked about him to people I met in a vague kind of way. "My friend and I always say this," or, "My friend would love that."

I sat on a park bench and watched other tourists wander the streets, holding up yellow cans of Águila beer like torches lighting their way to an experience. Pigeons filled the park almost as profusely as vendors, who were ready to sell you anything from turquoise rings to ice cream.

Bird chirps, ice cream bells, fountain splashes and the broken Spanish of drunk foreign exchange students all made a rich, organic orchestra that I preferred to the tired tunes on my phone. Here, I didn't need anything but what was right in front of me.

"What are you writing?" asked a skinny, freckled boy on the bench across from me.

"Just a diary." I smiled. Without my face buried in the phone, implying that I had more important things to do, random people were approaching me a lot more.

"You want some rum?" He and his buddies were drinking straight from the bottle at eleven in the morning.

"Sure." Why not? Where did I have to be? I finished my *tinto*, the ubiquitous sugary black coffee sold on every Colombian street corner, and I let them fill my plastic cup with rum. I shivered as I drank it back in one shot.

By now, the old me would have posted a whole slew of photos and hashtags. #MorningWorkout #SexySwim #Rum-Breakfast #PeacefulPark #SpanishArchitecture. I had assumed it would be hard not sharing all these new experiences, but, surprisingly, I didn't miss it. I thought back to sage advice, again from my childhood friend Bri, when she and I toured San Francisco last summer.

"Bri, can you take my photo in front of the bridge?" I had asked. #BayBridgeView.

"Take my photo with this cocktail. And our oysters." She sighed and set down the oyster she was about to eat. #HappyHour #Oysterdisiac.

"Pose with me. We need to show us together. Come on, just one." #Togetherness.

"Ew, these candies are gross. Let's take a photo making gross faces. Oh, it didn't turn out. It's not cute-gross but more like gross-gross. Let's do it again." #NastayCanday.

"Erin." Bri interrupted my madness. "Some things can just be for you."

"You're right." I turned off my phone and guarded it away deep in my purse as we continued our walk toward Pier 39.

At Pier 19, I doubled over with pain from a disabling ache in my lower back.

"Erin, are you okay? What's wrong?" Bri touched my back and bent over to look at my face.

"It's this UTI. It's not getting any better. My back hurts so bad. I'm sorry, but I don't think I can walk anymore."

"Erin, that's your kidneys. That's serious. We're taking you to the emergency room."

Half an hour later I was laid back on a hospital bed, where, sure enough, they confirmed a spreading kidney infection. I framed the photo to feature my bright-green sneakers and matching hospital bracelet. #EmergencyRoom #StillStylin.

I was sick, and my kidneys were the least of my problems. But here in Colombia, phoneless and fully present, I was healing.

"Hola." A baby-faced Colombian man in a tight red tee approached me. "I've seen you walk by here a few times. Can I help you find something?"

"No, I'm not lost. Well, I'm lost, but it's okay." I smiled.

"I'm Leo." He held out his hand.

"I'm Erin. Nice to meet you."

"I saw you pass by here a couple of times, and I couldn't take my eyes off you. You're gorgeous."

I laughed. I was wearing an oversized, saggy-butt pair of

khaki shorts and no makeup. He didn't laugh but gave me sultry eyes. If any girl out there needs a confidence boost, go to Colombia, where the men spit compliments like baseballers spit sunflower seeds.

"Um, thank you," I said, still laughing, disbelieving.

"Look, my band is playing tonight at Media Luna bar. Do you want to come?"

"You're in a band? Cool. What do you play?"

"African drum." I sure knew how to pick 'em. Tour guides, lifeguards and drummers, oh my. "Right now I'm headed to rehearsal, actually. You want to come?"

"Sure," I said. I followed Leo through the winding streets, into an abandoned building, up two flights of rickety stairs and down a wooden sagging hallway where I started to have second thoughts about the safety of following a flirtatious stranger. I was about to run the other direction, when he pulled open heavy, wooden double doors to reveal a bright-colored, co-ed decoupage of Caribbean characters tuning their instruments.

I settled on the love seat against the wall, sipping on a Club Colombia beer, and I prepared myself for a mediocre display of teenager-esque, garage-band strummings. Leo sat down at his drum and winked. What followed was pure magic.

Leo drummed an energetic, Caribbean beat that seemed to come from deep inside my own chest.

A petite man with deep dimples and big round eyes sang an unfailing, heart-melting tune.

A light-black woman with blonde, tight ringlets gathered into a multi-colored scarf clicked her minarets and convulsed her hips Shakira-style.

A tall, thick man with a broad nose and sideburns strummed the bass.

A skinny kid with spiky hair and one lazy eye pounded at the keyboard.

A handsome hippie with a five o'clock shadow and bad teeth leaned and swayed with his blows on the sax.

I sat there, dipping and bobbing my head to the beat, inspired and scribbling fast in my journal to capture the pounding in my chest, the admiration I felt for their skill but more so their passion. Instead of becoming part of my Facebook timeline or my Twitter feed, this moment was becoming a part of my soul.

As I watched them, with their eyes squeezed closed like believing children in prayer, tapping their feet and feeling their souls, I thought that perhaps art is the way we feel closest to God. They were just rehearsing, like I was just journaling, but that is when the real feeling comes, when it's for no one but you, to save your soul, and maybe for a tourist girl you picked up on a street corner and would like to impress.

They all looked like tortured souls, undulating between ecstatic joy and a melancholic comedown at the conclusion of each song. Was it because, in our art, we see glimpses of God's glory and then have to return to a normal state, comparatively torturous? I knew it to be true, from my own experience. We do see God's face in those moments, when we're spilling ink like blood, when we're dancing, when we're banging on our big red Caribbean drum. But then it ends, and that highest high is followed by the lowest low. God is gone.

22

BLACK MARKET FLECHA

I stared at my impotent iPhone, willing it to speak up already and tell me what to do today, who loves me, who I am, what I'm worth, the meaning of life. But, as I stared at it, lying on the chipped white windowsill in my bedroom, its hard case impervious to the healing breeze blowing in and tickling my face with my hair, I remembered that nothing was coming. No text, no email, no Facebook message was going to save me, so I started on the path of trying to save myself. I crawled onto the crisp light-blue sheets of my single bed, sat cross-legged, closed my eyes, and I was still.

In my silence, I overheard my roommate Beni laughing on Skype with his long-distance girlfriend. "I love you more," he cooed.

"No, I love you more, handsome."

A feeling of deep jealousy came over me. I want to talk to the one I love. But I can't. I can't because I'm doing this stupid, meaningless experiment and—the real truth hit me —I can't because he's married and he doesn't love me. I can't because I'm completely alone and I have nobody to call.

I had been hesitant to get a Colombian phone, for fear that it would provoke the same obsessive patterns from my past, but as things stood, no one could get a hold of me without taking a bus to my apartment building, talking to reception, calling upstairs and crossing their fingers that I would be home, which I usually was not. My goal had been to quit my addiction to media and Adam, not become a crazy lonely hermit lady. I decided it was time to get a simple little flip phone, so new friends here in Colombia could reach me. I could also make phone calls in case of an emergency, but I would not allow myself to go down the slippery slope of text messaging.

Not wanting to spend much money, I took a taxi to the center and wandered into the people-packed twists and turns of the Black Market, not just a concept but an actual locale I had been directed to for finding a used (perhaps stolen) phone.

Old men sat at school desks lining the row and focused on repairing switchboards, watch cogs and any other trinket that could be re-tooled and resold.

Young men leaned against buildings and cat-called me as I walked by. The old men did it, too, when they looked up.

"Psst. Psst. Nena. Nena. Nena." *Baby. Baby. Baby.* They were persistent in their psst-pssting.

"La más bella que he visto." *The most beautiful I've seen.* A man slithered far too close to my face.

I picked the scrawniest, most innocuous character of the bunch and asked, "Hey, um, where can I buy a phone around here?"

He jumped to and smiled. "I'm Elkin." He held out his hand. He looked about twenty-two, a bit chimpish with his high full cheeks and short teeth. Harmless.

"Hi, I'm Eva." I still gave him my safety name.

"I'll show you." He took off, taking sharp turns down a series of narrow alleys while I shambled behind, keeping my eyes on him and my hands on my pockets in the crowded marketplace.

We emerged from the shadowy aisles to the other side, where he sidled up to a booth and leaned on the glass display case and said, without making eye contact, "Hey man, Carlos, you gotta phone?"

Carlos pulled out a basic dumbphone, which they called a *flecha*, arrow, "because any Indian can have one." (I know, it's offensive. It's what they said.) It had sand in the button cracks, rusty auxiliary plug-ins, and a few of the buttons didn't work. Perfect, I thought. No temptation there.

Elkin's payment in orchestrating the deal was my phone number, which I couldn't say I didn't have since he had just helped me procure one. I thanked him and weaved my way out of the congested labyrinth back to the main road where I could orient myself by the spire of the yellow clock tower.

As I walked, I pulled Juan's phone number out of my pocket and programmed it into my new old phone, punching the name in rotary style. J. tU. A. mN. Save. Phew, that was a lot of work. I hadn't had a phone like this since 2003, my first year at university. I looked down at the phone and debated calling him but put it away.

23

MEDIA NARANJA

"*Alguna carta para 402B?*" *Any letter for 402B?* Antonio ducked to look in the cubby and shook his head. Two weeks had passed, and still nothing. I had already sent Adam three letters.

In the center, there is a triangular park across from the clock tower with a row of corrugated tin stalls lining one of its three lengths. I passed through the green iron gate to investigate these hovels that I thought were homeless shelters, and, instead, I found a nerd and writer's greatest pleasure. Books! Every single one of the shacks, for two city blocks, sold books. Literature books, text books, philosophy books, poetry books, children's books. I wished I could tell Adam, now, and not three weeks later when a letter might arrive. I took my time, strolling and examining the Spanish titles for one I might recognize.

About a third of the way down the row, a husky Afro-Colombian man with a chipped front tooth stood and approached me. "Have a seat, beautiful," he said, in Spanish, gesturing for me to sit at a school room desk. "Have a drink with me."

I accepted, and the man, who introduced himself as Hector, did a jumping jig and ran to get two Club Colombias, the other local beer, which he delivered with a bow.

"What are you doing here? Are you on vacation?"

"I live here," I said.

"Do you want to go out sometime?"

"I hardly know you," I said, though I considered saying yes, because his jocular, exaggerated manner made me laugh.

"That, beautiful, is why we should go out," he said.

"Tell me about yourself. You sell books. Do you like to read?"

"I don't really read." He shrugged and grinned.

"How can you recommend a good book to your customers if you haven't read them?"

Again he shrugged and grinned, showing his endearing chipped tooth. "What do you do, princess?"

"I'm a writer," I said, "So I like men who write and read."

"Well, I write a little bit," he said, stretching his fingers out in front of him.

"Is that so?" I smiled and crossed my legs, ready for the show.

"In fact, I've written a bit of poetry, just now, inspired by you."

"I can't wait to hear it."

"Okay, okay." He held his hands up, palms out.

"Your eyelashes,
Are like trampolines,
On which I bounce,
Dying for your attention."

I laughed. "Not bad. Great imagery."

He grinned. "Another beer?"

"Sure," I said, as I would say more and more with each day of this Caribbean laid-back lifestyle.

Hector fetched two more beers and sat opposite me, crossing a leg and leaning back. "You know, I think you may be my *media naranja.*"

"Media naranja?" I knew the words, *orange half,* but I didn't catch the meaning.

"It's a saying in Colombia. We say, 'I'm looking for my other orange half,' my soul mate."

"I like that." I looked down and smiled. Hector was fun, but he was definitely not my media naranja. Juan was great, maybe an orange segment, even. But Adam. Adam was my media naranja.

I thanked Hector for the beers and walked another third of the way down, choosing a stall at random to pop into and see what they had. As I scanned the wall of books, two jumped out at me, *One Thousand and One Nights* and *The Divine Comedy.* They were Juan's favorite books he had told me about, one from his childhood and the other of philosophical importance. It had to be a sign. I pulled up the one number I had programmed into my phone and hit *Llamar.* The phone rang, and I held my breath.

"¿Aló?" he answered, and my heart thumped.

"Juan. It's Erin."

"Hey can I call you back?"

"Sure," I said, hanging up, disappointed. He must be with one of his "amigas," I thought.

I walked the hour back to my apartment along the beach, craning my neck at every lifeguard tower and checking my phone every minute.

This flecha, as basic as it was, was just as detrimental as any of the other media I shut out of my life, because I was already looking to it constantly, insecurely, hopefully, obsessively, waiting for a white knight to come riding in or something to save my soul, to make me whole. Just then, the phone rang. I watched it ring, and I wanted to let it keep on ringing, to prove to myself that I was strong, that I was thinking independently.

"Aló," I answered, acting indifferent.

"Aló hermosa, ¿cómo estás?" *Hello beautiful, how are you?*

"I'm good," I said. He's not for me, I thought. He's a player. Whatever he asks, whatever he offers, turn it down.

"Would you like to go out tomorrow?"

"Yes." We made plans for the following evening, and I made plans to learn from my lessons.

PEACE-BOMBS AND LOVE-HATE

J uan and I walked along the top of the Spanish wall that
surrounds the historic center.

"This city is so romantic," I said, looking out over
the yellow-lit cobblestone streets below, at the couples
making out in alcoves cut into the wall. "If you can't fall in
love here, you can't fall in love anywhere."

"In Havana you can," he said, and my heart turned
inside-out. "I've heard it's even more romantic than here," he
continued, having no idea of the nerve he had just struck.

Juan kept talking, telling me the history of the wall built
by the Spanish to protect them from pirates, but my mind
may as well have been that pirate ship struck by a cannon
ball, doomed, sinking down into the sea of Adam. I wished
he were there, walking that wall with me, not talking about
boring history but about words and literature and inspiration and purpose.

We stopped at a popular local hangout, a section of the
wall that locals call, "Café de al Lado," *Café On the Side*. It was
located just outside Café del Mar, an overpriced restaurant

that no average Colombian, earning five hundred dollars a month, could afford to frequent.

Colombia is a country where the disparity between rich and poor is sharp, partially due to its narcotrafficking past and the riches that came of it, for some. But a beautiful thing about Colombians is they always make the best of their situation. Juan and I joined the many couples and friends who come there to Café de al Lado to drink cheap booze and eavesdrop the live music from the fancy joint next door.

Juan lifted me onto a cannon and poured me a plastic cup of wine. Our dates were always "a lo pobre," *as the poor do*, but he won me over with charm, "a lo latino," *as Latinos do*.

"Why did you move to Cartagena, if your family is in Barranquilla?" I asked him.

"I used to be very involved in politics," he said. "We protested for change and for peace, and, while in the U.S. your government lies to you, in Colombia, they kill you."

"What do you mean?"

"They kill you. If they don't like what you are doing. They have paramilitaries who do it so no one knows who's to blame. One day, a group at the university was making *papabombas*."

"What are papabombas?"

"Potato bombs. You take a potato, for weight, and then you add some gunpowder and a coin. You wrap all of that in aluminum foil, and, when you throw it, the coin and foil make a spark and ignite the gunpowder, making a small explosion."

"You were protesting for peace and you threw bombs? That doesn't make a lot of sense."

"We tried protesting peacefully, but the police will hurt

you, so we had to protect ourselves."

"Okay, go on. So what happened?"

"One day, some kids from our group were making papabombas in the university baseball dugout, and then, someone, a paramilitary, threw a grenade in there and killed all of them, eight kids."

"Were they your friends?" I asked.

"Some of them."

"I'm so sorry."

"Me too. After that, I thought it would be a good idea to get out of town. If you're involved here, if you make waves, they're watching you and, like I said, they'll kill you."

"Are you in any danger now?"

"No, I'm fine. It was a long time ago. But that is why I really want to study rights, to be a lawyer so I can help this fucking country have peace." He talked like a man who really cared, and I knew he loved his country very much, though he said he hated it.

The music from the café picked up, and Juan pulled me in close to him and twirled us around in *merengue* circles. I giggled and kissed him. He was fun. He was exciting. He was hot. But something felt off.

The wind started to pick up, so we found shelter behind a rampart and sat down on the cold stone ground.

"We need to do more writing," Juan said. "I need to practice."

"We do. What topic do you want to write on next?"

"Hmm, you choose."

"I know," I said. "How about something that seemed bad at first but actually turned out being good, for the best?"

"That's a good one. So tell me when that has happened for you."

"Oh, well I can't tell you now. We're going to write about it."

"We'll write about something else. I want to know the answer."

I knew, right away, exactly what it was, but I didn't want to say. If writing, I could think for a while and come up with something else that wasn't the real thing. I sat silent for several awkward minutes. "What's yours?" I said, trying to flip it on him.

"No, that's not fair. I asked you first."

I breathed in hard and back out. I was always a terrible liar, so I told him the truth. "Well, there was this...this thing. I was kind of...in love."

Juan furrowed his brow and looked down at the ground, nodding his head. It was too late now, so I kept going.

"I was in love, but the guy didn't love me back. He was married, actually. And, I thought I wanted it so much, that there was nothing that would make me happier, but, as it turns out, him not wanting me was a good thing. Because I'm here. Because I got to meet you." I threw in the last line to lessen the blow.

Juan kept nodding and biting the inside of his cheek on one side. "Are you still in love with him?" He asked the worst question you can ask a terrible liar in love. I thought of my public relations training, of all the ways I had learned to tap-dance around topics and answer without answering.

"I am," I said.

He breathed in through his nose, looking straight ahead at nothing, and exhaled hard.

"Well, that's complicated." In that moment, by the way it affected him, I realized that Juan actually cared about me. I gave him a hug, because I saw his vulnerability for the first time. He hugged me tight and rubbed my back softly, telling me without words that it was all okay, and we kissed. Ever handsy, he slid his hand up my skirt.

"Let's go to the hotel," I said, conceding what he had wanted for the past two weeks, since our first date.

We held hands, and he steered me through narrow alleys and turns, directly to a hotel in the center. I wondered how many times he had steered girls here before. We climbed three flights of stairs past dirt-streaked walls and he psst-pssted at the girl in the closet-sized reception room to get her attention.

"Good evening," she said.

"One hour, please," Juan said, pulling out his wallet.

"One hour?" I felt like a whore.

"Oh, you want to sleep?" He seemed genuinely surprised.

"Um, yeah."

"Okay, one night, please." He changed the order, and she handed us a key and a couple of crunchy towels.

When we got to the room, he faced me, brushed my hair out of my face and kissed me. He lifted my shirt up over my head and unhooked my bra with one swoop.

"Turn off the light," I said.

"No." He smiled and kissed me, running his hands over my bare back. I hugged around his waist and reached up under his shirt, feeling his warm, strong back.

"What do you want from this?" I asked.

"I want us to be *novios*," he said, meaning boyfriend and girlfriend.

"I want that, too," I said, but what I really wanted was to still be valued after the act.

He took off his shirt and threw it to the side. He picked me up and laid me down on the taut, white sheets. I felt a combination of desire and fear. I wanted him, but I didn't want to be left alone after, cold and unwanted.

Afterward, we laid down to sleep, the real test of intimacy. I had learned that anyone could be sensual in the heat of raging hormones and the promise of sex, but when it came to sleeping, that's where real intimacy was expressed. I faced him, smiling, not expecting anything more, and he pulled me in tight to his chest. He kissed me on the forehead and wrapped his arms and legs around me like he never wanted to let go. And he didn't.

In the morning, we went for a typical Colombian breakfast, a deep-fried *arepa* paired with sugary juice from a street cart. He continued his squeezy, oozy affection, and I reveled in the Colombianness of it all, walking along the cobblestone streets, holding hands while he called me *mamacita*. I'd forgotten about Adam, about media, about time. Oh shit, the time.

"What time is it?"

"Only nine."

"I have an interview with a sailing company at ten. I have to go."

"It's right around the corner. You have plenty of time."

"I can't go like this!" I looked down at my white miniskirt and low-cut tank top. "It's for a job, to sell tours for them. I have to look professional."

"You look good," Juan said. I would soon learn that, like most things in Caribbean Colombia, dress code was not so much code as flow, swaying to the rhythm of life like our hips to the thumping salsa beat at 4 a.m. on a Tuesday.

Juan kissed me goodbye, over and over and over...

"I have to go!" I pulled away laughing and hailed a taxi home to change my clothes and clean up fast.

I got out of the taxi, ran up the steps to the lobby, stopped at the front desk to ask, "¿Alguna carta para 402B?," ran up the four stories to my floor, pushed the door in to the apartment, slowly, as though somehow slow entry might prevent mama Dolores from judging my promiscuity. I stripped off last night's clothes, took a five-minute shower, threw on a dress and cardigan, put on some blush and eyeliner, brushed my hair, grabbed another taxi and arrived at the sailing company with two minutes to spare.

A blue-eyed Spaniard greeted me. "Buenos días."

"Buenos días. ¿Laura está aquí?" I asked for the owner whom I had arranged to meet.

"No, her dad's in town, so she stayed home today."

I breathed in through my nose and exhaled out hard. "Okay, thank you."

As with dress code, time and commitment were loose concepts in Colombia, so I went with the flow, bought a mango and wandered around. Back inside the walled city, near the clock tower, I paused to laugh at a group of six gringo boys falling off turquoise cruiser bicycles with baskets on the handlebars.

One of them, a short, fit, strong-jawed guy about my age with straight black hair parted on the side, stabilized himself and faced me. "Uahhh dónde café?" he asked in broken Spanish, assuming I was Colombian.

"Those bikes are cute," I said in English, laughing. "Follow me. I'll show you where to find coffee."

"Aw man, you speak English? Awesome!" Derek, the leader of the pack, mounted his bike and the six of them followed behind me as I guided them several blocks to the Juan Valdez café by the university. They were Navy seamen at port for the day, searching for souvenirs and fun, as seamen do. I helped them place their complicated orders for ground and bean coffee to take home to their wives whom they claimed were friends. Souvenirs done. Now fun. They insisted on compensating me with shots of tequila at one in the afternoon.

I led them to Getsemaní, a more run-down neighborhood just outside the fortress walls and one of my favorite places in the world. While within the walls everything is prepped for pamphlet photography and cruise tourists, Getsemaní has graffiti on its walls, prostitutes on its steps and fire in its belly. Literal fire. At night, the backpacker-artesans who need to make a few pesos spin and spit fire in the central Plaza Trinidad, alongside local families, unicyclists, contortionists, bracelet makers, break dancers, and stray dogs hoping to catch a few mouthfuls of *patacones*, the fried plantain pile-up sold at street carts.

Back in the 1500s, when the wall was built, the rich Spanish conquistadors lived inside the walls and their slaves lived outside it, in Getsemaní. For many years, the neighborhood was crime-ridden and trash-laden, but now it was a vibrant local hotspot with colorful murals and hipster cafes.

The boys and I popped in and out of several bars there, and, by 4 p.m., we were all buzzed on cheap rum, tequila and hot sun.

A skinny, sweaty Afro-Colombian man began to follow us down the street. He wore a grubby button-up shirt that hung open to show a distended belly, and, despite a lanky stumble, he was catching up to us, since six tipsy sailors on bicycles don't move too well, either. He came up behind Derek and started gyrating his hips and grinding on him.

"What the fuck are you doing, man?" Derek jumped backward.

The man didn't say anything but leaned one arm on Derek's shoulder and suckled at a plastic water bottle one-third full with a chunky, yellowish substance. He wiped some of the yellow stuff on a dirty blankie hanging over his shoulder.

"Get the fuck offa' me," Derek yelled in his Boston accent, pushing the man's hand off. "I'm gonna clobber ya."

I tried to intervene with Spanish. "Please, don't bother them. They're just trying to enjoy the city."

The guy was too drugged to hear me or to care. He took some more of the paste and wiped it on one of the other guy's backs.

"Oh, that's it. This guy's gonna be bloody." Derek pushed out his chest. We could have increased our pace, turned a corner and moved on, but Derek wanted a fight, maybe from all those regimented days of testosterone building up at sea. He pushed the man, who stumbled backward.

"¿Necesitan ayuda?" *Do you need help?* asked a round-faced, light-black Colombian man with acne scars and a papaya-colored polo shirt.

"¡Si, por favor!" I said. *Yes, please!*

Jorge put his hand on the druggie's shoulder, said two words, and the druggie left without question, never to be seen again. I had to know. "¿Qué le dijiste?" *What did you say to him?*

"It's easy," Jorge responded in perfect English. "All that needs to be said is, 'Déjalos tranquilos.' Leave them in peace."

"I appreciate it. I tried everything, but he wasn't listening."

"You have to make eye contact with him, let him know that you respect him, and he'll respect you."

Respect the drugged loser who was harassing our group? I thought it absurd. I would later learn that the substance the man was sniffing in the water bottle is called *boxer* and that people inhale the fumes to help them not feel the pangs of starvation. I realized that when Jorge said respect he meant empathy, which I felt in great measure now knowing more of the story. Everyone makes the choices they do for a reason, even if those reasons are ones we can't initially see or understand.

The Navy ramblers had to leave to return their rented bicycles, but Jorge invited me to stay and celebrate his thir- tieth birthday with him and a multi-cultural crew of amigos, who should be arriving soon. The intriguing couple I met that night would change the entire course of my adventure and perhaps my life.

I was immediately drawn to Megan, to the openness in her expression and posture. She had round, smart brown eyes and an intriguing balance of feminine and masculine, with her soft curly brown hair in a ponytail that exposed the shaved lower half of her head. In Maine, she had left behind an emotionally abusive ex-husband and her own accounting business to live a simpler, happier life sailing the Caribbean and working in tourism.

Her Swedish boyfriend Filip was her perfect comple- ment, tender-eyed and twelve years her junior, with a style I'd describe as middle-aged American hippie. He was pale and blonde, with a mis-buttoned cotton shirt that exposed a pot belly. While one side of his mouth smiled, showing yellowed teeth, his light blue eyes always looked a little sad. I think they were made that way just for Megan, showing her the compassion she needed and deserved.

Together, Megan and Filip were co-captains of a cata-

maran owned by Renato, a stout old Portuguese man with
Coke-bottle glasses, an abundance of hair coming out of one
nostril, and wavy hair sticking to the sweaty sides of his
weathered face.

I loved how in Cartagena one could find such an array of
backgrounds and back stories. My hometown in Southern
Oregon was so homogenous, all having lived some variation
of a few plots, but here I was always excitedly learning about
new cultures and corners of the world.

At the bar, Jorge bought a round of drinks, Megan
bought a round, Renato bought a round, and round and
round we went, until we were all hugging and swaying and
laughing in the street. Filip entertained us with his patented
"Swalsa," a Swedish salsa jig with lots of squatting and elbow
action.

"Erin, we want to make you an offer," Filip said. "We
really like you. You're pretty, you're positive, you like the
Swalsa."

"I do love the Swalsa."

"We want you to be our primary agent in Cartagena.
We'll give you a twenty percent commission to sell catamaran tours to backpackers, from here to San Blas.[1] We're
just getting started and need someone just like you."

This was exactly what I'd set out to do this morning, at
my canceled interview, and now here it was falling into my
lap. I enthusiastically accepted and made plans to meet
them the following morning at the boat for a tour. I desperately wanted into boat world, and this was a fantastic start.

---

1. *Comarca de Guna Yala* is the official name for this region, formerly known
to some as San Blas.

25

BOATLANDIA

"Are you sure this is it?" I asked, when the taxi pulled up to a wall of cobbled-together scrap metal covered in graffiti. With a name like the Nautical Club, I had expected something fancier, dressed in my blue and white striped maxi dress with a side braid.

"Si. Club Naútica."

"Okay, gracias." I got out and walked the perimeter of the wall searching for an entry. A piece of the scrap metal opened, revealing a "door" held open by a thin Colombian man while two old white men exited.

"Hi," I said to the expressionless doorkeeper with protruding forehead. "I'm here to meet with Megan and Filip."

"What's the name of the boat?" he asked.

"I don't know. I'm meeting Megan and Filip. I'm working for them."

"I don't know them." He began to shut the door.

"Wait. Renato? Do you know Renato?"

"No." He shut the door.

I couldn't call Megan and Filip, because their phone had fallen overboard last week. I knocked again. The doorkeeper opened the door and stared at me.

"How about Jorge? You know Jorge? He works here, too."

"Those ladies down the street have Jorge's number." He gestured toward two middle-aged women sitting on the street corner selling llamadas, *phone calls*. He was about to shut the door again when Jorge came walking down the walkway of the scrap-metal fortress.

"Hey, Erin, what are you doing here?" Jorge gave me a hug and kiss on the cheek.

"I'm meeting with Megan and Filip, but this guy won't let me in."

"Come with me, darling." Jorge escorted me inside, and I shot the doorkeeper a told-ya-so look. He stared back, expressionless.

We walked the long wooden dock past everything from skiffs to superyachts, until we arrived at Tatiana, the catamaran named for Renato's daughter.

"You made it!" Megan yelled, in her usual posture of a wide strong stance. She was beautiful, in her cheap tattered bikini, her cheeks brown and her round eyes smiling.

"I'm sorry I'm late," I said. "I've been trying to get in for fifteen minutes."

"No worries! Come on over!" I really was the only person in Colombia who cared about punctuality.

A wooden plank secured by ropes bridged the two worlds, normalcy and Boatlandia, as they called it. I wobbled down the plank and jumped the three feet down into the catamaran.

Renato was inside, wiping sweat from his forehead and talking to himself in angry Portuguese. Megan leaned into my ear and held up her hand to whisper. "Just a warning. Anyone who has anything to do with boats is a little fucking crazy." I laughed now, but I would later learn this was dangerously true.

The boat, like Renato, was rough. Paint chipped and fell from the ceiling, speckling the crew members with white spots, like reverse dalmatians. Rotting fruits and vegetables leaked onto the galley counters. I was supposed to sell *this* for five hundred dollars a person?

"I know, it looks kind of rough." Megan read my mind, or maybe it was my face. "Renato just bought it, and we're fixing her up." She led me downstairs into one of the cabins, and, as soon as she opened the door, it reeked of sour sweat and unflushed turds. "It's very spacious," she said. I nodded, eyes wide, trying to see the positive she peddled.

We walked out onto the bow and, standing on that white fiberglass rocking cradle, looking out over the harbor and blue ocean, I found it. Crude and dirty cabins and captains aside, I wanted to be a part of this world.

"It's great," I said. "I'm happy I met you guys. And let me know if you ever need a deckhand."

26

AMIGAS

Two whole days had passed without hearing from Juan since our night together, so I decided to go get a coffee and pity myself. I walked the street, not the beach, to the nearest Juan Valdez café. I didn't want to pass by Juan's lifeguard friends as they ogled his latest gringa conquest.

I usually ordered a *malteada mocca*, basically a chocolate milkshake with a hint of coffee. Feeling fat and abandoned, I decided to choose something healthier.

I saw a pretty, tall-for-Colombia girl with thick brown hair stirring a chocolatey drink and approached her.

"Qué es eso?" I asked, in Spanish. *What is that?*

She looked at me with a look I had seen before, a look I had made before: deer-in-headlights language interpretation panic. Ah yes, a fellow gringa. I switched to English.

"Sorry, I thought you were Colombian."

"It's okay, I thought you were, too."

"What kind of drink is that?"

"Well, usually I get the *malteada mocca*, but I'm trying this because it has fewer calories. It's okay. It's no malteada."

I laughed. "I was doing the same thing. I always get the malteada but I was forcing myself to order something else."

"Oh my God, that's so funny."

"Do you want to talk?" I asked, sensing immediately that we could be friends.

"Yeah!" she said. "I'm Gina. I'll be sitting right outside."

I went to place my order, ruffling my fingernails through my hair for more volume and sucking in my stomach. I was slightly in love with the dreamy barista with the caramel-colored skin and never-ending eyelashes, even though the extent of our exchanges over the past couple weeks was always the same.

"Un mocca, por favor." *A mocha, please.*

"Si mi amor. A la orden." *Yes, my love. At your service.*

I found my new friend Gina at one of the round garden tables on the patio. Everyone who meets Gina describes her as glamorous, with her sparkly brown eyes, her strong Sicilian nose and waist-length wavy hair. I envied her perfect natural breasts, her long, olive-green dress with slits up the sides revealing toned thighs, her gold-hoop earrings—all so gloriously glamorous, a word I'm sure no one has ever used to describe me.

"Oof, that barista is the most gorgeous thing I've ever seen in my life," I said. (I had started using the interjection "oof" that *costeños* use with frequency.)

"Oh my God, Marvin? I'm in love with him," she said. "What an awful name though. Why does he have to be named Marvin?"

"Right? I always thought the same thing. His name doesn't match his face at all." We both laughed. We were going to be friends.

After talking for an hour, Gina's Canadian roommate

Rachael joined us, a petite twenty-two-year-old Nigerian-American girl with big doe eyes and Afro hair dyed brown. We all started to chat about the Colombian dating scene.

"I'm seeing someone actually," I said. "He's a lifeguard."

"Rachael knows a lifeguard," Gina said with that school-yard K-I-S-S-I-N-G tone.

"Oh, I know almost all of them," I said. "I work out with them most mornings. What's his name?"

"Juan Calderón," Rachael said.

My heart stopped. I had just decided to trust him, to sleep with him, two nights ago, and today he still hadn't called as promised. "That's who I'm seeing." My face and neck felt hot.

"I'm so sorry," Rachael said, her beautiful pitying eyes making it worse. "If it makes you feel better, he was supposed to call me today, but he hasn't."

"Yeah, he was supposed to call me, too." I wrapped my hands around my neck, feeling my heartbeat in my throat. "How did you meet him?"

"I was walking on the beach..." I didn't hear the rest. I wanted to vomit. This was his ploy. The sexy lifeguard-lawyer who doesn't have a girlfriend but has "amigas" and talks philosophy and draws you ever closer until you break and he bails. I tuned back in to hear the story so I could plot my revenge.

"To be fair, he didn't actually do anything wrong," she said, trying to calm my ire. "His friend Humberto tried to hit on me, and I said I didn't speak Spanish so he'd leave me alone. Humberto went and got Juan to have him translate."

"Okay. So how did you two end up exchanging numbers?"

"We were just talking about how I'm new here, and he said he could show me the city."

"I hate him," I said.

"I hate him, too," Gina chimed in. "I don't even know him, and I hate him."

"He hasn't actually done anything wrong," Rachael said. "He wasn't even flirting with me."

"He offered to give you a 'city tour,'" I said. "A city tour is not really a city tour. How do you think he and I started dating?"

"Let's do this," Rachael proposed. "Let's hang out together tonight, and if he calls either of us, the other one will pick up and scare the shit out of him."

"I like that."

"This is so crazy," Gina said. "That you two would meet like this by coincidence and it would come up like it did."

"It's either a crazy coincidence, or he does this to every fucking gringa wandering down the beach," I said.

That night, Juan called neither of us, and I imagined he was onto his next conquest, probably at the same sketchy one-hour hotel.

———

The next morning, I woke to my flip phone ringing. Juan. I took a deep breath and let it ring. No way, nuh-uh. If he thinks I'm going to talk to him after he ghosted me for two days, after he tried to bang Rachael, he has something else coming. Why would I? Why would he? I wonder what he wants. I looked down at the missed call. Maybe I should call him back to give him the chance to explain, or to lure him in and exact my revenge. Yes. I hit the call-back button.

"Hey, nena, how are you?" he asked.

"I'm fine. You?"

"I'm good. Today's my day off."

"Oh. Good for you. Why didn't you call yesterday?"

"I had to organize some things," he said. Were those things per chance a girlfriend and a litter of illegitimate children? I breathed in through my nose and closed my eyes.

"Do you want to get together tonight?" he asked. That night I had planned to go to salsa class with Rachael and Gina. This was perfect, far better than a phone ambush.

"Yeah, I do, sweetie." I turned my voice sweet and coaxing. "But I met some girlfriends, and we have plans to do salsa class tonight at eight. Why don't you meet us there?"

"Okay, sounds good," he said. "I can't wait to see you."

"I can't wait to see you either, darling."

That night, I put on a white tank and a flowy coral skirt that would sway and flip as we moved our hips to the sexy salsa. I wanted to look hot, to make Juan regret his man-slut stupidity.

I met the girls in the Quiebra Canto bar where we gulped back some *cuba libres* to loosen us up before the lesson. We were still drinking and giggling at the bar when someone put his hand on my lower back, and I turned, expecting to find Juan.

"Hello ladies, I am Lorenzo, your salsa teacher," said a dark-skinned, solid-bodied man with intense black eyes.

We all immediately shifted into flirtation mode. Rachael held out her delicate hand and smiled a cute, tongue-biting smile. Gina hunched her shoulders forward, showing off her assets. I used my kill shot, a permeating I-may-be-your-soul-mate eye contact that, from his reaction, seemed to do the trick.

"Me gusta tu mirada," he said. *I like the look in your eyes.*

Lorenzo was patient with our giggling, his English was perfect, and he explained things so well that, by the end of the lesson, we were doing the Cuban and Colombian shuffles and spinning round like semi-pros—when he led, that is. I forgot all about Juan and, when I did remember him, as the class wrapped up, I hoped he wasn't coming. I didn't want his slutty butt to ruin my Lorenzo mojo.

"Lorenzo, we're going to forget all of this," Gina said. "Can you write it down for us?"

"I have a pen and paper," I offered.

"Sure, ladies. I would love to." He wrote a list of all the steps we had learned and signed it with an extravagant signature, a heart and a "muak," the Spanish sound for a kiss.

"Will you keep it forever?" he asked, as he handed my journal back to me and made bedroom eyes.

"Of course," I said. Semi-drunk promises made to twenty-four-year-old, sexy salsa teachers don't count.

Juan had not shown up, of course, but I was having such a great time with the girls that I didn't care. We headed for a restaurant in Getsemaní and, as we walked that way, Juan called.

"Where are you?" he asked in an irritated tone.

"Well, you are more than an hour late, so we left."

"Where are you now? I came all the way to the center to see you."

"You came an hour late. We're in Getsemaní, at Este es el Punto restaurant en Calle de Tripas y Medias."

"That's far away," he said.

"It's not far. It's like four blocks away."

"Okay, I'll come over there," he said.

"Okay, see you soon." I hung up the phone and started plotting with the girls how we were going to act and what we were going to say when he saw us sitting there at the table together.

"I'm a terrible liar," Gina said, stressed. "This is going to be so awkward. I can't take it."

"I am too," I said. "I'm going to the bathroom. He should be here any minute."

I took my time in the bathroom and, when I walked out, it was perfect. He and Rachael were hugging hello as he saw me approaching over her shoulder, his face twisting in confusion.

"Hi sweetheart!" I said. "You two know each other?"

He looked between us, completely confused, and Rachael jumped in. "Yeah! We met last week. This is, wait, is this your boyfriend?"

"Yeah, this is Juan!" I said. " How do you two know each other?"

"Ohhh my gosh!" she put her hand on her chest. "This is sooo funny!" We both were terrible actresses, compensating with over-enthusiasm.

Juan looked back and forth between the two of us and then to his two buddies, Omar and Martín, who had accompanied him to the restaurant. Everyone looked confused. Gina, still sitting at the table, rested her head on her hand to hide her face.

Juan hugged me and kissed me sensually on the lips. He knew he was in trouble, and now he was the one over-compensating. "You two know each other?" he asked.

"Yeah, babe, this is my new friend I was telling you about. Rachael. She's an English teacher."

"Yeah, I know she is," he said. "I told you about her, remember?"

"Umm, no you didn't."

"Yeah. Rachael the English teacher? I showed you her text last week and said you could talk to her about teaching English here? Remember?"

Oh shoot. I did remember, now. He did show me that when we were cooking dinner at Beni's house last week, which would have been right after they met.

"You didn't make the connection?" he asked. "An English teacher named Rachael?"

"No, I didn't even think of it. There are lots of English teachers here. What a coincidence."

He narrowed his eyes and cocked his head. "Are you sure you didn't know that we knew each other?"

"No hon, I had no idea." Again, terrible liar.

Our food came, and everyone was quiet. We three girls leaned over the table and whispered amongst ourselves in fast English we knew they wouldn't understand. The three guys sat in chairs to the side of our table doing the same in Spanish.

"This is so awkward. They know we're talking about them," Gina said.

"They're talking about us, too," I said. "What did he do when he saw you? How did it go down?"

Rachael gave the play by play. "He was walking toward the restaurant and when he saw me, it looked like he was going to just keep walking. But I called out to him and said 'hi.' I asked him what he was doing, and he said he and his friends were just going for a walk."

"He didn't say anything about meeting his girlfriend," Gina added.

"Yeah, I figured," I said. "He did tell me about you before. But he obviously wanted to take you out. But I don't know if that's so bad. At this point, I would go out with hot barista boy or hot salsa boy if they asked."

"Well he's what I expected," Gina said, leaning back, crossing her arms and glaring at him. "Mr. Suave."

"Yeah, he's smooth," I said, looking over at him as he laughed with his boys, running a hand over his hair.

"And hot," Rachael added.

"He is hot," I said, mashing my lips together in defeat.

THINGS I HATE ABOUT ME

A pparently, Juan's hotness overshadowed his hoe-ness, because we continued dating. We also continued our workouts coupled with the writing exchange to help improve his English and my Spanish.

Today's topic, which Juan came up with, was, "Something you don't like about yourself." As I sat with pen paralyzed, bleeding ink into one spot on the page, I felt so frustrated. There was a long list of things I hated about myself, ample subject material, and yet I couldn't write it. I was afraid of choosing the wrong thing, afraid of doing it poorly, afraid of disclosing my true thoughts. I hated that afraid feeling, and there it was, my topic.

February 20, 2014 [translated from Spanish]
I'm going to tell you something I have that no one knows, the thing that I most hate about me that I think is the root of all the other things I do not like.

It's something paralyzing and appears in every hour of

the day, in the least expected moments, stupid
moments, and I can't explain it.

As I hang my clothes, cut a mango, get into the ocean,
write this fucking page, do all of these basic things that I
know that I can do, I am overtaken by ANXIETY.

My chest feels tight and I almost can't breathe sometimes. But no one would know it, even those who know
me well. They say, "You are so daring, so fearless, so
outgoing." "You have so much courage, traveling as
you do."

There is a veteran of World War I who said, "There can
be no courage unless you are scared." Well, I guess in
that sense I am very courageous, because I am always
scared.

I suppose, beneath that anxiety, there is an even worse
defect: pride. Like everyone, I don't want to appear
stupid, and, for that reason, I don't do anything.
If I don't do anything, there is nothing to lose (or so I tell
myself). If I simply sleep, if I don't make any move, I
can't fuck everything up.

If I spend the day chatting about trivial things with
comfortable friends, I can't ruin anything.

But I also can't build, grow, improve.

It is for that reason that anxiety is the root of every other
thing that afflicts me.

I am fat because I have anxiety at seeing what is possible (or not possible) for my body.

I am lazy because I have anxiety at going in the wrong direction and wasting time.

I am dependent because I have anxiety that I can't do it on my own.

I am a procrastinator because I have anxiety that I might do it imperfectly and, therefore, I find distractions until the last minute.

I am quiet because I have anxiety of using the wrong words and expressing myself poorly.

And the worst part of all is that, inside of me, I AM NOT any of these things: fat, lazy, dependent, procrastinating, quiet.

To the contrary, I am energetic, independent, effective, athletic, outgoing.

Anxiety, fear, is bullshit. It is a mythical monster that only exists in the mind and has nothing to do with reality.

This is the year that I kill the monster. It is not going to eat me if I have the flavor of sweat and determination.

"You really feel like this?" Juan asked. I felt embarrassed, like he must think I'm crazy, pathetic, weak. It made me feel like a freak that he seemed to relate in no way whatsoever. I was about to back-pedal, but I instead decided to keep speeding downhill.

"I do."

He puckered his lips and nodded. I proceeded to read his essay, about hating his small feet which are out of proportion to his tall body. I missed Adam. We really knew how to be miserable together.

28

A SURPRISE

Two weeks later, a surprise arrived.

"Hermanita, there's something downstairs for you in the lobby," Beni said, as he hung up the phone on the kitchen wall.

"I wonder what it could be."

It had been a month since I'd arrived and, while I had sent fifteen or so letters out into the void, I had not received a single one. But if it were a letter, they would simply put it in the box for us to pick up with the bills and other mail when we stopped by. It was bigger than a letter. My mind spiraled up and down and all around. This is it. This is it. Adam is here. He realized he can't live without me and he's here. No, he wouldn't come here. Remember the 'trust me'? But if he changed his mind? What else could it be? He came for me. He's here, this is really it. This is the moment when he tells me he loves me and he always loved me and he will love me forever.

I went into the bathroom and did my makeup fast. I tried to fix my messy, wispy hair. I pushed my boobs up as high as they would go in my racerback tank. I rode the elevator the long four floors down, assessing myself in the mirrored wall, heart about to explode.

I stepped out of the elevator, the moment of truth, the moment that would confirm that my heart was right all along and that the pull I felt toward him really was the universe showing me the way to my other half, my media naranja.

A mailman waited by the reception desk. He handed me a mid-sized envelope, and, though I was disappointed it wasn't Adam, I felt so excited to finally receive mail that I hugged and kissed the man on the cheek. This meant that many more, from Adam, should be arriving soon.

I opened it up to find a Valentine's Day card from my dad and stepmom with melted chocolates mashed inside. I laughed. My pothead pops must have thought this would be a good idea. These were the beautiful nuances you couldn't receive in a Facebook message. A card took time. The senders had to select it and touch it and think of you for more than two fleeting seconds. They had to fill it with their unique handwriting and touch it with the oils on their skin and imbue it with their energies. It had to be walked to a mailbox or post office then sent across two continents. It felt, and was, so much more special than the multitudinous, mindless messages that we fire off with more immediate digital media.

This particular card probably made it because it had chocolates inside and, therefore, required a customs claim form on the front. I wondered if others would make their way as well, and I lamented all the potentially lost words, words that could change everything.

29

RUM AND TONGUE

"Okay, nena, I told my mom we'll get in later tonight. What time are we meeting at the clock tower?" Juan asked me for the fifth time. We and my new friends were headed two hours east to experience Carnaval, the pre-Lent, four-day drunken festival celebrated famously in the town of Barranquilla, where Juan's family also lived.

"Four," I said. "The bus is going to be there at four. Don't be late. I don't want Gina, Rachael and all their teacher friends to be waiting on us."

"No, don't worry nena. I'll be there. I have to run an errand at the university, but then I'll be there."

I, too, was running the risk of being late. It was 3:30, and I had just started packing. I heaved a wad of clothes from my dresser into my backpack, uncertain whether I had anything that made a complete outfit. I dumped travel toiletries on top, rounded the room pulling chargers from plug-ins and crammed the tangled mess into a top pocket. 3:45. I heaved my pack onto my back, gave Beni a kiss on the cheek bye, and waited for the slowest elevator of all time.

I would normally get to the center by *colectivo*, the Cartagena taxi system where you hold up one finger to share a ride with strangers and pay one-third the price, but time was of the essence, so I paid the whole six thousand pesos (three U.S. dollars) for the private taxi and checked the time as I climbed in. 3:52.

The taxi pulled to the curb by the clock tower at 3:59, and I scanned the large plaza in front for backpacks but only saw the usual vendors with their styrofoam ice chests and 8x10s of local islands to entice tourists into a tour.

I got out and stood awkwardly alone with my giant pack. Where were they? I wasn't upset with Gina or Rachael or any of their friends for being late, but Juan promised me he would be here. I called him, and he didn't pick up. I called again.

"¿Aló?"he answered.

"Where are you?"

"I'm on my way, nena. I just have to run by the university and then I'll be there."

"You haven't gone by the university yet? You're already late. Just come right here."

"What time does the bus leave?" he asked, again.

"They said we should all be here at four. And it's already ten after."

"Is everyone else there?"

"It doesn't matter. You are supposed to be here. I'm here. I busted my ass to get here."

"Okay, okay. I'm on my way."

I took off my pack and crossed my arms. Three other gringos with backpacks walked toward me, looking lost.

"Hey! Are you guys Gina and Rachael's friends?"

"Yeah," said a skinny, unfriendly Australian guy with Harry Potter glasses. "Is the bus here?"

"I've been watching for it. I haven't seen it yet," I said.

"I'll call," said a pretty, plump Mexican girl named Ariceli with stunning emerald eyes and dark lashes.

While Ari called the bus company, I called Juan. "Everyone's here. Where are you?"

"I'm on my way. I'm dropping this library book off."

"Your errand was a library book? Well hurry." I hung up, fed up. Gina and Rachael arrived in a taxi and, now, everyone really was there. Except Juan.

The sprinter van pulled up to the curb, and we all crawled in. The university was a ten-minute walk away. He should be here any minute. I could stall for a few minutes. The van started rolling.

"Wait, wait. We have one more coming," I advised, in Spanish.

"Doesn't matter. We can't stay parked there or the police will give us trouble. Tell them to meet you at our office in Marbella."

I called again. "Juan, where are you? The bus left, but they said we are stopping at their main office in Marbella so you can take a taxi there."

"You *left* me?" he said, incensed.

"It's 4:40. I told you to be there at four."

"You said the bus would be at the clock tower."

"Yeah, and you said you'd be there by four. Just take a taxi and meet us at Marbella. It's not a big deal."

"Ugh. Put me on the phone with them."

I passed the phone to the employee in the front passenger seat, embarrassed, and listened to her argue with him and tell him what I told him, to take a taxi the five minutes to Marbella where we would wait for him.

Once at the bus company, we waited ten minutes, and I dialed Juan. "Juan, where are you? This van is leaving now."

"Oh, so you're going to leave me again."

"They said they have one seat open in the next van, which is leaving in half an hour. I reserved a seat for you in that one."

"Wait for me. Go with me in that one."

"Did you hear me? They have *one seat*. It's Carnaval time. Everything is booked."

"What about my seat on your bus?"

"Are you here? It's leaving now. Don't you get it? Just go in the next bus, and I'll meet you in Barranquilla." I hung up and vented to Gina at my side.

"He's being such a baby about it," she said. "He could've been here by now if he weren't throwing a massive fit."

"Seriously. You know what, I'm going to tell him to forget it. I'll have more fun with you guys, anyway." Without Juan, I had no place to stay, and every hostel bed in Barranquilla was booked, but I didn't care. I called him back.

"Juan? Don't bother coming. This was supposed to be fun, and this isn't fun."

"You don't want me to come?" he asked, shocked.

"I think it's for the best."

"You want me to cancel on my mom? She's expecting us."

"Yeah."

"Okay. Fine."

I didn't want to meet his mom, anyway. Juan and I had only been seeing each other a few weeks, and I didn't feel like being a dancing circus bear for a woman he himself had described as cold and judgmental.

A few minutes later, I received a text on my flip phone, in English.

JUAN

I'm sorry. I was really bad. Enjoy the
Carnaval. Sorry.

If I could text, I would have written back to Juan, "It's okay," and the next thing you know, I'd be getting off the bus and waiting for him and meeting his mom and all his brothers and aunts and uncles and cousins and we'd get drunk together and we'd have make-up sex and I'd get knocked up and have a little Colombian baby and I'd be happy for about two years until he would cheat on me with one of his "amigas" and I'd have to move back to Oregon and live with my mom and beg a job back from my old company and live the life I had escaped for a brief stint, the life I never wanted. One text message—one simple, two-word message —could be the difference between two entirely different destinies.

I chose silence.

When we got to the hostel my friends had booked in Barranquilla, it turned out that there had been a clerical error and they didn't have beds either, which made me feel better about my own lack of lodging. At least we were all homeless together. The hostel owner felt bad about the mistake and connected the six of us with his neighbor Arturo, who had some extra beds in his house across the street.

The gray-haired neighbor with cataracted, tired eyes looked at us with disdain and didn't speak a word but motioned for us to follow him. He guided us across the street, through an iron gate onto a tiled patio where two other old men sat in plastic chairs and commented in Spanish.

"You find yourself some gringos, Arturo?"

He laughed. "Yeah, I'm gonna make some money." They all laughed.

He opened a second iron gate and showed us into a long, narrow corridor with shelves full of art supplies and walls featuring art from floor to ceiling. We walked past three elderly Colombian women watching *telenovelas*, soap operas, on a fifteen-inch tube TV and stepped up one step into another long room that had three twin beds, a double bed and a hammock.

"Here it is," he said.

"Cuánto costa?" A blonde, German med student from our group asked the price in poor Spanish.

"Twenty a night," he said. "Each." He looked at us smiling, trying to contain his excitement at the six-teated cash cow standing before him. I was about to contest the dramatic price gouge.

"We'll take it," said Dr. Presumptuous, speaking for all of us without consultation. Damn. Now I couldn't even negotiate down to the five dollars each it was worth, but I probably couldn't have anyway, given our untenable circumstances.

So, there we were, six gringos sleeping in an art gallery. Arturo gave us one key to share between us and promised that no one else would have access to our space. We hid our key on the patio, in a bag full of potting soil, and we hit the streets.

The whole city was alive with color and costume. Locals wore homemade t-shirts splattered with sequins, ribbons and paint. Women and girls were dressed up like what they called the *Negrita Puloy*, the Carnaval mascot with spiral curls, bright red lips, a red polka-dotted dress and matching headband.

We walked one block to a market on the corner and were drawn in by warbled Latin music blasting into the street and a lively, drunken crowd singing along on its patio. We joined in, grabbing the one remaining plastic table and squeezing around it.

My friends snapped pictures with their phones, posing together and trying to capture it all for Facebook. I captured it for me. I felt the drips of condensation rolling off my cold beer and onto my calves. I heard the shuffle of dominoes, the coos of Colombians crooning Marc Antony, the claps to the Latin rhythms. I watched the rainbow of triangle flags above us palpitate with the cool breeze bringing evening. I smelled the charcoal and grease from chicken burgers grilling on the street cart parked nearby.

We covered the bright red plastic table with empty beer bottles and walked back to our art gallery to get started on the rum.

When we got back, a friend of one of the teachers had arrived there at the gallery to meet us. He was from Boston but had lived in Barranquilla for three years and, well, it didn't really matter. Within minutes we were sitting on the hammock making out. I can't remember the conversation exactly, but I think it went something like:

"Hey, what's your name?"

"Blah, what's yours?"

"Erin, nice to meet you." (Insert tongue in mouth.)

"Who wants a rum and Coke?" Gina asked, and all of us, now ten travelers strong, raised our hands. We polished off a *pipón*, the mid-sized bottle of Medellín Rum, in ten minutes. We mixed more rum and Coke into plastic to-go bottles.

My nameless makeout buddy led us about ten blocks to a massive street party, where thousands of locals and hundreds of tourists were crammed together sweating and drinking and dancing. Everyone from our group sifted off like puffs of flour getting kneaded into the sticky dough of Colombian Carnaval.

Five hours later, I found myself coming out of a blackout on the steps of a dark warehouse, not remembering anything from the past few hours.

"Marijuana never works for me," I told two unknown Colombians and a gringo sitting by my side when I began my return to consciousness.

"This will," promised the stranger.

It was at that moment that I looked around and realized that I had absolutely no clue where I was. The thousands of people who had previously populated the streets were gone, and it was just me and these three nefarious characters sitting on a concrete raised patio on a street covered in Carnaval carnage.

I began to panic. I didn't know where my friends were. I didn't know where the art gallery was. Unlike a hostel, it had no name or signage to guide a taxi to. I hadn't even noted what street it was on. I had no phone on me and no contact info for anyone I was with. I took another hit of the joint. It was dumb, but it was the only thing I knew to do in my drunken, panicked state.

Then, like an answer to an unspoken prayer, Jesse, one of the teachers from our group, appeared out of nowhere, his lanky figure rocking side-to-side toward us with the halo of his giant straw sombrero framing his goofy, grinning face.

"Whoa, hey!" he said in his surfer voice.

"Jesse, thank God you're here. Where are we?"

He took the joint from me and took a drag as well. "I don't really know," he said, jutting his chin forward and back in a sliding nod.

"It doesn't matter. At least we found each other," I said.

"Totally. Let's go walking and I'll bet we find it. We'll look for something familiar."

We wandered the deserted streets, littered with empty cans and trodden decorations, until we ran into a group of policemen.

"What are you two doing out here?" a stout, aggressive officer asked. I worried we were about to be victims of the common sport of framing tourists for bribe money. Just last week, Gina and I had run to the aid of our two gay friends who were wrongfully accused of committing a lewd act on the beach. In the end, we paid the cops the equivalent of twenty U.S. dollars to make it go away. This, tonight, wouldn't even require framing. Jesse and I reeked of booze and illegal marijuana.

"Yeah, officer, we're lost and I dunno if you can help us, like, find our place. It's kind of near this market." Between Jesse's clueless appearance and shitty Spanish, we were certain to be taken advantage of. I jumped in with my sweetest Spanish.

"Sorry to bother you, gentlemen. We got separated from our group, and we were hoping you might help us."

"You speak Spanish well," he said. "You Colombian?"

"Thank you," I replied, instinctively pulling down my short skirt. "And yes, my parents are Colombian." I lied, hoping a claim to shared nationality might endear them to us.

"Hmmm," he said, looking down his nose at us and rubbing his round chin. "You shouldn't be out here. It's really dangerous. People get mugged down here all the time. You're lucky you ran into us."

"Can you help us find our place? It shouldn't be too far from here."

"What's the name of the hostel?"

"It's a private home."

"What street is it on?"

"We don't know." We sounded like idiots, probably because we were. "It's across from a hostel," I added, as though that might help when there are hundreds of hostels in Barranquilla, the fourth largest city in Colombia.

The cop hailed a passing taxi and leaned in the passenger window to talk with the guy in mumbled Spanish. I imagined what they were saying: *These idiots are completely lost and probably have lots of money. Drive them out to that abandoned lot and take 'em for all they've got. Hold onto the girl and we'll be there in twenty to do a gang bang.*

"Alright," the officer said. "He's going to drive you around the area, and you can look for something familiar." He rolled his eyes and exhaled as he drummed his belly with his fingers. We got in, despite my worries, and I wondered if floppy, skinny Jesse could protect me with the Tai Chi he blathered on about earlier that afternoon.

We drove around as the meter racked up pesos, and Jesse and I stared into the dark looking for any landmark, any little sign that might cue our memories.

"There! Look!" I pointed to the market where we'd started drinking in the afternoon. I thanked my writerly attention to detail, having journaled earlier about the rainbow flags and chicken cart. "Let us out here, please."

We made it. We walked the one block to our art gallery, dug for the shared key in the bag of potting soil, and tripped over shoes and bags in the dark until we found open spots among the drunken gringos sprawled like sea lions.

"¡Hay más gringos aquí, Arturo! ¿Cobraste a todos?" *There are more gringos here, Arturo! Did you charge all of them?* An old Colombian woman in a floral dress stood in the middle of our room and yelled in a high-pitched crow over her shoulder.

"Ya vengo, ya vengo." *I'm coming, I'm coming.* Arturo entered the room and stood by her side, counting us. I pretended to be asleep, hoping they'd go away, but he came to my hammock and pushed it to wake his resident interpreter.

At the same time, two new tourists whom we didn't know came traipsing through our room to the bathroom with towels over their shoulders.

I sat up in my hammock. "Arturo, what are they doing in here? You said no one would come in our room."

"Tranquila, no pasa nada," he said. *Calm down, nothing happened.* How could I argue with that? Colombians say "no pasa nada" a lot, whenever someone apologizes or worries unnecessarily. "Sorry I bumped into you." "No pasa nada." "Sorry I spilled your drink." "No pasa nada." "Why are all these strangers in our private room?" "No pasa nada."

The three women who were watching soap operas yesterday ducked under my hammock and turned on the TV at a blaring volume. The German doctor and his girlfriend were naked on a pile of couch cushions on the floor. Gina was covering her head with a pillow. Ariceli was sprawled out and drenched, for some reason. More gringos whom we didn't know stepped over our friends and bags to make a line for the one bathroom. I exhaled and laid back down, surrendering to the craziness. It was parade day, the real start to Carnaval, and things were about to get a lot crazier.

Once again, our group dispersed when we hit the crowd, but I was at least able to keep track of glamorous Gina, floppy Jesse, and a petite girl called Natalie with striking blue eyes. The four of us shoulder-squeezed our way through the glitter-dusted, black-painted, foam-spraying, hip-bumping, champeta-dancing, rum-drinking, loud-laughing, falling-over crowd.

It was a narrow passageway along the sidewalk, lined with vendor carts cooking grilled meats to our left and the backs of tall bleachers to our right, looking down on the street where the parade would soon begin.

They had blocked the view through the bleachers with cardboard so that anyone who wanted to see the parade would have to pay the sixty thousand pesos, about thirty U.S. dollars, for a seat. We wanted to save that money for the thirty beers it could buy us instead, so we kept pushing our way along the sidewalk, looking for a gap through which we could see the big event.

We walked a long time without finding an opening, and, seeing through the few slivers in the impenetrable fortress that the parade had begun, we decided to approach one of the many scalpers who had been trying to sell us seats all along. A thick, short Colombian man held out a fan of tickets.

"Just sixty thousand each, these are in the VIP section," he said.

"Where?" I asked. "Point to where they are." He pointed across the street to a small set of bleachers.

"Those are good seats," Gina commented, in mumbled English, so he wouldn't know we were interested.

"I don't want to pay sixty thousand," Natalie said. As English teachers there, they were only making about seven hundred U.S. dollars a month.

"Me either," Jesse said.

I turned back to the scalper. "We'll give you one hundred thousand for all four of them."

The man laughed at me. "You will not get tickets for that price."

"Then we won't get tickets," I said, shrugging, and all of us did the notorious haggle walk-away.

"Wait, wait, wait," he said, chasing after us. "I will give you a very good deal. Four VIP tickets for one hundred twenty thousand."

"What do you think guys? Can we do thirty thousand? That's fifteen dollars each."

"I'm not doing it," Natalie said, crossing her arms. She was impressively tough with her sweet mouse voice and waif frame. "The parade has already started. He's going to make nothing or what we offer him."

"Let's do it," Gina said. "We're here to see Carnaval. It's only fifteen dollars."

I was inclined to agree with Gina. I looked between the three of them to gauge where they stood. Traveling with people was so much more complicated than going alone.

"I don't care," Jesse said, relaxed in his decision-making as he was in his sauntering.

"I'll pay yours," said Gina to Natalie. Gina was always

incredibly generous and also hated conflict, no matter how mild.

"Okay, deal." Everyone compiled their pesos to buy the tickets from the grinning scalper. "What's your name?" I asked him, just in case.

"Raúl," he said.

"Ok, thanks Raúl."

We rushed over to an entry spot where we showed a cop our tickets, and he let us pass into an area packed with other neck-stretching people trying to catch a glimpse of the glitter and glam. Since our seats were on the other side of the street, we pushed toward the metal rails that contained the herd from the street.

"Perdón. Perdón," we said as we pushed through. A short woman with orange-bleached hair, black-painted eyebrows and a sequined red hat elbowed me hard in the side.

"You can't just push in front of us," she said.

"We're just trying to cross the street, to those bleachers," I explained. "That's where our seats are."

"They are not going to let you pass, honey," she said, with 'honey' sounding anything but sweet. "No one is allowed to cross once the parade starts."

We had been conned. Raúl, or whatever his name really was, surely knew what we did not, that the tickets across the street were useless now that the parade had started.

I, as interpreter and mediator, felt guilty for losing these poor English teachers' hard-earned pesos, so I committed myself to finding a way across. I burrowed through people toward the rail, where I popped out like a meerkat and tapped a tall police officer on the shoulder.

He turned around and, *Perfect*, I thought. He was about

my age and handsome with kind brown eyes. I looked up at him with watery eyes. "Sir, can you help me?"

"Of course. What can I do?"

"Someone sold us these tickets for those bleachers there across the street." I pointed. "But they tell us we can't cross now that the parade has started."

He looked up and all around, adjusting his duty belt. "Let me see if I can do something about that," he said. He walked over to the other cops lining the rail and leaned in to confer with them.

He came back, holding his belt and looking at the ground. "It's true. It's very hard to get across once the parade starts."

"We were conned," I said, arching my eyebrows in distress.

"It's terrible, how people take advantage of tourists," he said, shaking his head. "Would you recognize the guy if you saw him again?"

"Definitely," I said.

"Okay, let's go see if we can get your money back."

Jesse, with his limited attention span, had already wandered off by now, so we three girls stomped behind Officer Pérez searching for the con man. Pérez stopped to question other scalpers, who shifted uneasily and claimed that Raúl did not exist. It looked like we were going to be out our forty-five dollars, or forty-five beers, the more valuable of Carnaval currencies.

"Come with me," Pérez said, striding back toward the crowd we first found him in. He ushered us in front of him, holding his long arms out to the sides to protect us from jabs and shoves. We passed the woman who had elbowed me, and I looked back at her with a smug smile. No one allowed to cross, eh?

I figured Pérez was going to walk us across the street once there was a lull in the parade, but, instead, he pulled open the rail and led us to a front-row spot where only medics, officers and important-looking people were allowed. He introduced us to a woman I imagined was the mayor of Barranquilla, in her red suit with matching red lipstick and tight bun. She smiled and welcomed us to her city.

"You can stand here," Pérez said. We all started giggling with excitement. Standing right on the street, we could not get any closer to the action.

A twenty-foot-high, flower-covered float with pink confetti bits flying glided by with a Colombian woman dressed like Glenda the Good Witch in her puffy pink ball gown.

"That's the Carnaval queen," Mayor Red Suit leaned in to tell me.

A painted pride of lions came running and roaring, leaning in to growl at us, clawing and posing for pictures in front of Gina's Canon camera.

"They think I'm a reporter!" Gina said. "They all keep stopping to pose in front of me!"

"This is perfect," Natalie said, accepting a flower from a passing clown.

Creamy-skinned Colombian women spun in their sparkling Cinderella skirts. Fedora-wearing men drank from plastic cups and sweated out the alcohol. Drag queens in sequined gowns and feathered headdresses swiveled their hips. Skinny boys in white linen and sombreros banged their cow-skin drums. Egyptian pharaohs and their Cleopatras shone gold in the hot sun. A band of gorillas squatted and screamed. Famous Colombian musicians floated by singing, as people behind us covered their mouths and squealed with excitement for the local celebrities. Painted *negrita puloys* with fruit piled high on their scarved heads curtsied. Nearly naked, big-breasted *garotas* shook their thick booties and tail feathers. *Señoras* in white and red multi-tiered ruffled dresses with flowers tucked behind their ears smiled and proved that wrinkles can be beautiful.

It was too much, too brilliant, too goosebump-giving to bear.

MISSING SOME-JUAN

In my marriage, I could say that I loved John, but I found it interesting that I never once *missed* him. I would travel for work conferences for a week or more sometimes, and, when I was gone, I didn't want to call him. It was a chore rather than a delight, and I did it only out of wifely duty. But when Adam was on vacation for a week, I felt like my heart was inside-out. I felt what it really was to miss someone, to ache for his presence, because he unlocked a piece of me I felt I couldn't access without him.

Before I met him, I was paralyzed by fear of failure. I couldn't speak sometimes for fear of using the wrong words. I never wrote for the same reason. Something about Adam made me feel it was okay to stumble and fail, like he would still accept me, because he understood that there was more intelligence and potential trying to break through to the surface. So, Adam was not the only person I ever loved. He was more important than that. He was the only person I ever missed. I missed him every day.

"¿Alguna carta para 402B?" I asked the front desk, part of

my new daily routine. The answer was the same as always, a slow, pitying head shake.

I hadn't received a single thing since the melted chocolates from Dad. If the Colombian postal system, my main form of outside communication, didn't work, maybe I needed to modify the rules.

However, I knew if I gave myself an inch I'd take a mile. If I allowed email, soon enough Adam and I would be bouncing back and forth messages in real time, and I would be back to depending on him for every little thing from basic decisions to my self-worth.

Since Juan and I broke up a couple weeks earlier, I had gone on two dates—one with Lorenzo the salsa teacher and one with Marvin the dreamy barista. Lorenzo spent the whole date bragging about his choreography accomplishments and calling me the cringey nickname "Kitty Baby" (based on me leaning into him for more head-petting).

Marvin also had two marks against him, having disclosed he had a kid and, worse than that, he was part of the same multi-level marketing scheme as my host mom Dolores. One more date and he surely would be trying to sell me the same bullshit creams and supplements that she always did.

I didn't think I missed Juan, but I kept finding myself frequenting the places I thought he might be. I arrived at Plaza Trinidad in Getsemaní and found a spot to sit on one of the sagging, slanted benches. I scanned the stone steps in front of the yellow cathedral, hoping to glimpse him among the crowd. Why hadn't he called me? Was it really over? Was I too hard on him in the Barranquilla bus mishap?

If Juan were here, I wouldn't have to face the blank page, in my journal or myself. He would squeeze me tight and

nibble my ear and dip me back and tell me I'm *hermosa*. I
wanted to text him desperately. But just as I had to ask
myself why I reached for media, I had to ask myself why I
reached for men. I reached for their attention in the same
circumstances—when I was feeling lonely, bored, purpose-
less, insignificant. I resolved to feel all of it, if only for the
night.

The next morning, my phone rang. It was Juan.

"Hi, how are you doing?" he asked.

"I'm great. How are you?" I stood and paced the outdoor
patio of the Juan Valdez café where I had been writing.

"I'm fine, thanks. How is your writing going?"

"Great. I've been doing a lot more of it lately."

"I'm happy for you," he said.

"Thanks," I said.

"Um, I was wondering if, maybe, I left my lifeguard
whistle in your bedroom."

"No, I don't think so. I haven't seen it."

"Oh, well, I just thought I would check."

"Okay. I'll call you if I see it."

"Okay. Take care."

"Take care." I hung up and wondered how much a little
plastic whistle could be worth to warrant that awkward
phone call. How would he have left his whistle? That didn't
even make sense.

That evening, I went to the movies by myself, which
made me feel an odd combination of independence and
patheticness at once. My few friends in Cartagena were busy.
Gina's parents were visiting, so she was touring with them.

My roommate Beni seemed to be interminably chatting on Skype with his girlfriend. I had ignored all texts and phone calls from Lorenzo and Marvin, uncertain of how to proceed with either.

Even in my media-obsessed days, I never, ever took my phone out during movies, because I considered it the rudest of offenses, worthy of a targeted glare. However, this time, about two hours into the film, something compelled me to take a look. Juan had sent me a text two minutes earlier, in English:

JUAN

I miss you. Sorry

My chest thumped. I slipped the phone back into my purse and watched the rest of the film, though distracted, considering what I should say or do, if anything. I asked myself if I just missed the attention, the kisses, the warmth and affection. But I could get those anywhere.

I really missed Juan. I missed his raspy voice and funny laugh. I missed his patient, professorial way of teaching everything from swimming to strategies for successful socialism. I missed being sporadically spun round in circles and dipped back for impromptu kisses. I missed sitting in his lifeguard tower and watching the sunset. I missed drinking cheap red wine out of plastic cups with him and his friends in the plazas. Perhaps more than Juan the person, I missed Juan the lifestyle. "He's *so* Colombian," Gina used to say. It was true. If Colombia could be wrapped up in a handsome package and personified, Juan would be it.

By the time I arrived to Plaza Trinidad, I had decided. I called, but he didn't answer. I tried again. And again. I wanted to let him know I missed him, too. After six weeks without sending a single text message to anyone, I caved and sent a single word:

Llámame.

Call me. I justified that one text would be alright if it contained only logistical coordination and no emotion. My phone rang.

"¿Aló?" I answered.

"Aló," he said, with hardly any breath. He sounded terrified.

"I miss you, too, Juan," I said, walking around the side of the church and holding my hand over one ear to muffle the noise of partying, transient backpackers.

"You do?" He regained some composure.

"I do. Come see me, please."

"Where are you?"

"Plaza Trinidad."

"I'm in my house, and I have to work early tomorrow."

"Oh. Okay, well, it's okay. We'll see each other later." I bowed my head and paced the stone landing.

"I'll be there," he said, his voice restored to the confident, raspy tone I loved. "Wait for me there."

"Are you sure?"

"Yes. I want to see you."

One text and one taxi were all it took to jump in again, to allow all my existential distress to be soothed by handsome distraction.

TYING THE KNOT

I want to ask you something," Juan said one night, as we sat on a bench in Plaza de los Coches, behind the clock tower where he took my picture on our first date. "Something I need an answer to."

"Ask me."

"Tomorrow. I want to do it 'a lo latino.'" *As Latinos do.*

"No, come on, ask me," I begged, plying him with kisses and playing with the curls on the back of his head.

"No, no. Tomorrow, I promise. Okay?"

"Okay." I smiled and leaned my head on his shoulder while we talked more about philosophy.

After a while, I looked at the time and pushed my phone into his face. "It's tomorrow! You have to ask me."

"What?"

"It's after Midnight. It's now tomorrow. You promised you'd ask me now."

He sighed. "Okay, if you insist. But remember I wanted to do it right."

I was really curious now, and a little concerned. What

did I do? Did he hear about my makeout session with what's-his-tongue at Carnaval? What intense thing did he need to know?

"Ask me."

"Erin." He looked into my eyes. "Will you be my girlfriend?"

I didn't see this coming. I gave him a hug, looking over his shoulder at the cobblestone ground and holding on for minutes, buying time, as I remembered the last time I felt precisely this way—the night that John proposed.

"Yes," I said.

Juan kissed me, and I smiled. It was not lost on me that the name Juan translates to John in English.

Juan and I walked along Calle Venezuela, the main street that passes in front of the clock tower, and we stopped at a large tree with hundreds of little white tags hanging from its branches. I looked at the placard beneath it.

Yoko Ono Wishing Tree

"You write your wish on a tag and hang it here," Juan explained.

"Let's do it," I said, pulling a piece of paper from my journal. I ripped it into two rectangular pieces and handed one to Juan, with a pen.

We both bent over and used our knees for support. I wondered if he was going to write something romantic, a wish about me. I wished I had a wish about him, but I knew what I really wanted, and I wasn't going to waste my wish.

He took my paper from me and, without looking at it, he tied mine and his together on a tree branch with some string he had scavenged.

"You're not going to read it?" I asked.

"Can I?"

"I want to read yours."

I stood on my tiptoes so I could reach the paper and twist it to see:

Deseo paz para Colombia y para mi alma.
I want peace for Colombia and for my soul.

"Which do you think will come first?" I asked.

"I think they'll come at the same time," he said.

He reached up and turned mine to see:

Deseo siempre ser quien soy y seguir mi intuición.
I want to always be who I am and follow my intuition.

I didn't care what he thought of it. It was *my* wish, and just writing what I really wanted instead of what I thought someone else wanted to hear was a huge step in fulfilling that wish.

He put his arm around me, and we kept walking. While I congratulated myself for writing my real wish, I also considered the irony that it was physically tied to Juan's wish.

AWARE WE GO

"Let's get one more drink at Mamallena," Gina said. Juan and I agreed. Despite a feeling of being smothered, I had been his girlfriend for one full month now. I knew how to do smothered. I didn't know how to do alone.

The three of us walked down Calle Media Luna to the backpacker bar and stepped into the crowded loud space to order our usual two-for-one mojitos. As I pushed toward the bar, a familiar woman's voice called to me.

"Erin!"

I turned around. It was Megan, from the catamaran, pushing past people to give me a sweaty hug. I thought she would be upset with me, because I had quit being their agent as soon as I realized I hate selling stuff, but she seemed happy.

"We've been looking all over the city for you!"

"You have?" I liked them, too, but I hadn't thought much about them since I quit. She dragged me back toward the entrance where Filip leaned against the open doorway, drinking a mojito through a straw.

"I found her!" she yelled. Now I was intrigued. She squared off in front of me with that wide stance and started explaining. "We have this friend Carl who has a sailboat. He is looking for someone, a female, to sail with him to Bocas del Toro, Panama, on a three-month trip, and we immediately thought of you. It's a great opportunity. It doesn't pay, but it includes free lodging on the boat, food, drinks, and the trip, of course. He only wants a couple of hours of work a day."

Flags went up in my brain. Why did he want a female? What kind of "work" was this? I didn't need to ask any more questions.

"It sounds great, but I'm really just getting settled here. I have my boyfriend." I gestured out the door to Juan, who was talking with friends in the street.

"That's even better!" Megan said. "He said he would actually prefer a couple. I didn't know you had a boyfriend."

"Yeah, he's right outside." I grabbed Megan's hand and pulled her out the wide doorless entry to the sidewalk, where backpackers and locals spilled onto the street drinking and laughing.

"Megan, this is Juan."

"Hi Megan, nice to meet you," he said in his cute, over-pronounced English, holding out his hand. She shook it firmly, grinning.

I grabbed his forearm. "Hon, you want to go on a sailboat to Panama?" I was joking, since I knew he had to finish his law school thesis and find a job.

"Yeah! When do we leave?"

"It's for three months," I said.

"Sounds really good," he said.

"Well, there you go." I turned back to Megan. "I think we may be in."

"Oh, and here's Carl!" Megan spread her open palm toward a skinny, hunched man in a Hawaiian shirt walking toward us.

"Carl, this is Erin."

"Hi Carl, nice to meet you." I held out my hand. He took it but didn't say anything and looked past me to Megan.

"You got a light?" A cigarette hung from wrinkled lips under a coarse gray moustache.

Carl lit his cigarette and sat down on the cement stoop of a row house next to the bar. "Megan, this is my friend Angelique." He pulled a light-skinned Colombian girl about thirty years his junior down onto his lap. She smiled, showing yellowed teeth through at least three layers of dried-out fuchsia lipstick. She had a fake glittery flower pinned in her straight black hair and light blue contacts over round, googly eyes. She was too pretty a girl for Carl and too ugly a prostitute for Carl.

I crouched down in front of Carl and Angelique on the stoop. "So, Carl, Megan tells me you're planning a trip."

"Two years. I do a one-year circuit through the Caribbean."

"Wow."

"Meet me at the marina tomorrow and we can talk about the details." That was my cue that he didn't want to talk about it now.

"Okay, what time?"

"I don't know," he whined. "I get up at 4 a.m., so it doesn't matter to me."

Megan intervened. "Come around nine. We can have some beers and chat."

"Okay, we'll be there," I said, excited. I had wanted to be a part of boat world, and this was my chance.

That night, Juan accompanied me to my apartment, and we kissed in front of the door as he ran his hands up my shirt. "Can't I stay the night?"

"I think Beni's mom would freak out."

"I understand." We kept kissing and things heated up further.

"Okay, go wait in the stairwell, and I'll see if the coast is clear. We have to be so quiet."

"Okay." He smiled and sat on the stairs around the corner.

I peeked inside the apartment, and, seeing no one in the living room at 2 a.m., I waved him in and pushed him in front of me, through the front door and into my bedroom.

We made love, quietly, and afterward neither of us could sleep.

"I used to be with lots of girls," he confessed, "But that doesn't fill me anymore. It's like you told me about your brother and how he ate sandwiches every day in college, and then he didn't ever want to see a sandwich again."

I laid on his chest, a warm contrast to the air-conditioned room. "If they're all sandwiches, then what am I?"

He looked down at me and smiled. "Spaghetti Bolognese, of course." His favorite. We both laughed, and I bit his shoulder to stifle my laughter.

My alarm sounded at eight, and we both had to pee. I slowly opened my bedroom door, and Dolores was right there, facing me and the naked man sprawled on the bed behind me. I slammed the door fast, then cracked it open and turtled my head out.

"Dolores, you scared me. Sorry it's just, it's a total mess in there."

"Hmmm." She crossed her arms and popped a foot out to the side. Her tired, wrinkled eyes looked through me as she pursed her red lips.

"I'll be right out." I turtled my head back in and locked the door behind me.

"Shit," I whispered, turning around to warn Juan, who was already gone. We were four stories up, so I looked for him in the only place he could have gone, the closet.

In my room, there were built-in closets that spanned the entire wall opposite the bed, with a space in the middle for a TV and drawers. The closet on the left was stacked high with Dolores's things, and the one on the right held a few of my dresses and, now, Juan.

"Stay here," I said. "I'm going talk with her a bit to dispel any suspicion."

"Okay." He gave me a kiss and made himself comfortable.

I walked out in a pair of shorts and a tank top. "Hey, Dolores. Sorry about that. My room's a disaster."

"Oh, don't worry, nena. But while you're here, I'm going to take advantage and get into that closet."

I swallowed my tongue. "Um, oh, no, maybe, well, wait." I was making it worse. She had to be onto me. "Okay."

She followed me into the room, and I talked loudly to alert Juan. "So, Dolores, how did you sleep?"

"Good, thanks, nena." She approached the non-Juan closet on the left and unlocked the padlock holding it closed.

She slowly, slowly, slowly pulled everything out that was stacked from floor to ceiling.

Pillows. Fake flowers. Photo albums. Board games. Files. Stuffed animals. I backed away from her toward Juan's closet, crossing my arms and forming a human wall that I prayed she wouldn't pass. Dolores was delicate, paranoid and afraid of everything. She would have a heart attack.

I noticed Juan's unbuttoned jeans on the floor next to the bed and his shirt hanging over the top of my big red suitcase.

Dolores pulled out plastic bins, purses, children's toys. What if she wants to put some of this stuff in the Juan closet? Dear God, please don't let her go over there, I prayed. I pushed my suitcase in front of the closet, laid it down and leaned the lid against the doors, pawing through and pretending to look for the day's outfit. Please God, please. Don't let Dolores die by heart attack this day.

"Well, nena, I got what I needed." She held a single manila folder.

"I'll help you put everything back." I jumped to my feet and started gathering all the items on the bed into a sloppy wobbling stack. "I'll take care of all this. Don't you worry about it."

"No, no. I pulled it all out. I'll put it back," she said. She handed me a plastic bin. She passed me two throw pillows. She lifted a ceramic pot with fake flowers. Item by item, with excruciating slowness, we filled the closet back up. She wrapped the chain back around the closet door handles and shut the padlock.

"Gracias, nena," she said and walked out. I locked the door behind her and tiptoed fast to the other closet, where I pulled open the closet door to find Juan sitting naked in lotus position.

"What are you doing?" I laughed.

"Meditating. I had to stay quiet. I thought she was coming over here."

"Oof, so did I. I think she knew something was up."

"Well, we made it. I'm still exhausted. Let's go back to sleep," he said.

"Babe, we have our meeting at the marina, about the sailboat trip. But Dolores is still out there."

"Oh, shit. What do we do?"

"How about you sleep some more, and I'll go to the meeting and get all the facts for us." The truth was, I wanted to go alone. As much as I enjoyed Juan's company, and I was ready to do the trip together when I thought it would last three months, I wasn't sure I wanted to be crammed into a tiny cabin with him for a full year.

"Sounds good, nena." He collapsed on the bed and was asleep in minutes.

"¿Alguna carta para 402B?" I asked on my way out. Antonio bent at the waist to look in the cubby and stood back up, shaking his head.

"Okay, thanks Tonio." I ran down the building steps and grabbed a cab to the Nautical Club, where this time the dense doorkeeper let me pass without incident.

"Erin!" Megan greeted me. She held up her hand to her mouth and hollered, "Carl, Erin's here!"

I loved Megan. I wanted to be like her, and she made me want to sail so I could become as much a woman as she was. She didn't have a selfish bone in her solid sailor's body, and everyone who knew it either took advantage of her or worshiped her. She could scrape barnacles and she could bake banana bread. She was gentle and nurturing, but strong and able.

I wobbled down the plank bridging the dock to the catamaran, almost falling overboard into the polluted marina water, and I jumped the three feet down, nearly twisting an ankle.

On his own time, the only time he recognized, Carl came dawdling over in his board shorts. He boarded the catamaran by backing down the plank on all fours and stretching a skinny leg down to the platform.

"Beer, Carl?" Megan knew him well. She asked in such an inviting way, always hoping the person would say yes.

"Yes, please," he said as he slid onto the bench seat at the table on the aft deck. It was 9 a.m., and all three of them sipped on beers for breakfast.

Carl's unruly eyebrows sheltered kind brown eyes. He had a full head of salt-and-pepper hair with the texture and look of cockatiel feathers. His whole body was leathery brown and wrinkled, making his sixty-two years look more like seventy-five. His diet consisted of about ten cheap beers and three packs of Marlboros a day, leaving him only a small belly, a concave chest, a hunched back and skin-and-bone limbs.

"Well, there's not much to talk about," Carl said, taking a drink of beer and staring down at the table. "I ask two hours of work a day. You can do it whenever you want. You eat what I eat. If you want something special, get it. If you finish something off, replace it. Because if I go to my fridge and I'm feeling like some olives, I don't want to get there and for there to be no olives."

"Where all will you be going?"

"We're going to San Blas Islands, Red Frog Marina in Bocas del Toro, it's a very nice marina, Porto-bello, Provencia and San Andreas, Rio Dul-che, Isla de Moo-hair, Havana or Jamaica, I haven't made my mind up yet, the Virgin Islands, Puerto Rico and then back here to Carta-haynya."

My chest swelled at the list of tropical destinations I'd always wanted to see, mispronounced though they were.

"That sounds amazing," I said. I felt an overwhelming desire to do this, and a voice inside me said that I should do it alone.

"Your boyfriend coming?" Carl asked.

"We're not sure yet," I said. Initially, I never would have considered going on this trip alone, out into the open sea with a complete stranger. I had needed Juan to come for my safety, but after talking with Carl, I felt he was no threat.

"Well, you wanna see the boat?" he asked.

"Yes," I said, eager to see what could be my home for the next year.

Funny the small things that make our decisions for us in the end. As soon as I saw the skylight in my cabin, I knew I was going. I imagined myself out at sea, staring up at millions of stars, unobscured by pollution or city lights, and I gave Carl an enthusiastic, undoubting yes to the adventure.

What I did doubt was Juan. If he went with me, would I write? Would I learn to be a real deckhand, or would I depend on his strength instead? Would we continue filling every spare minute with kissing and canoodling? All of that was great, but something deeper was missing.

So, I lied to Juan, and I told him the truth. I lied when I said that it would be logistically impossible for him to go, that Carl insisted on leaving before Juan's law school thesis presentation next month. I told the truth when I told him that my intuition told me I should go alone.

He reached across the table at the restaurant where I broke the news, and he squeezed my hand, understanding and unphased. "You have to do what's best for you," he said. "We'll stay friends and keep talking."

I offered to pay for lunch, my idea of a consolation prize for his canceled Caribbean cruise, and I walked up to the counter. Patricia, the restaurant owner whom I'd talked with a few times before, glared at Juan over my shoulder with her intense, round eyes.

"I don't like him," she whispered, in English.

I laughed. "It's okay, Patricia. Don't worry."

"Be careful with him, nena," she said.

"Do you know him?" I asked.

"No, but I know his type."

I thought it was odd, and I would have shrugged it off as nothing if I hadn't already heard the same warning whispers before, inside my heart.

Carl wanted me to move onto the boat as soon as possible, so I could start learning the literal ropes. I agreed, so I also could see how it was living with Carl and have the opportunity to back out before we were surrounded by miles of water on all sides.

In our meeting, my intuition had told me that Carl was no threat. He was sixty-two years old, he barely ate, and he smoked three packs a day. I could take him. And he didn't look at me in that way.

Carl's wife Annie, the love of his life, died of lung cancer ten years ago. When she passed, he sold his trucking company and started sailing, embittered and angry at the fact that they had spent her final years trying every treatment under the sun instead of soaking up the sun together, enjoying her remaining time.

"You're going to help Carl find love again!" Gina said, and I hoped that might be true. I wanted it to be a beautiful story of two victims of heartbreak on the high seas, learning to live and love again.

Before I headed out into the receptionless void, I had to call Mom and Dad to let them know I was going away on a boat for a year with a stranger. I called Mom first, figuring she'd be the more difficult of the two to persuade that, yes, it was safe, and, yes, I would be fine, and, no, Carl was not going to throw my body overboard.

"Hi sweetie!" Before I could say anything about the trip, she started crying. It was the first time we had talked since I left Oregon two months ago. "Honey, it's so good to hear from you. I was just thinking of you. I had a dream about you last night. I hadn't heard from you these past couple of months, and I was so worried, but I had this dream that let me know that you were okay."

"What was it?"

"You were in the middle of the ocean, and you were so happy. It was kind of a dangerous situation, but you were so happy, and it let me know you would be okay."

Now I was the one crying. Aside from my intuition, I wasn't actually sure that, yes, it was safe, and, yes, I would be fine, and, no, Carl wasn't going to throw my body overboard. Now, with that one premonition from Mom, I felt certain.

"Mom, I am going in the ocean. And I am going to be so happy."

As I left the apartment, I asked one final time.

"¿Alguna carta para 402B?" *Any letter for 402B?*

"No, nena. Lo siento." *No, hon. I'm sorry.*

3

DOLPHIN OMEN

Carl and I sailed away from the fuel dock, waving goodbye to Juan, Megan and Filip. I had said goodbye to Gina the night before, at a going-away party on Carl's boat, where she generously gifted me a care package for the crossing with everything from sunscreen to chocolates for keeping me awake during night watch.

"Women either love or hate sailing," Carl warned. Just a mile out, with the wind in my face and my knees bent to sustain the dip and rise of the bow, I loved it. I wanted to be a sailor. I felt as free as the boat untied from its dock lines, and I couldn't wait to get out to the point of no return, surrounded by blue and yielding to the will of the sea, to God.

I was scared and exhilarated at once. I didn't know if I'd be able to handle it, if I'd get seasick or be strong enough to pull the lines or be a good enough swimmer to scrape barnacles. But more than any of those things, I was afraid of being alone, now truly unreachable by anyone, by Adam.

I had fantasized all this time about him turning up on my doorstep.

On the beach, with every shadow cast over my written page in the moonlight, I prayed it was his shadow.

When I walked home, I hoped to find him sitting on the front steps of the apartment building.

When he wasn't on the steps, I imagined he was standing inside the lobby, hands folded, anticipating my arrival.

When he wasn't in the lobby, I held my breath as I pushed in the apartment door, ready to see him waiting on the couch.

In the coffee shop, I sometimes thought I saw him, pushing in the door and coming to find me there.

It never ended. I was always waiting for him, always hoping for him. But now, he couldn't reach me if he wanted to. Out here, the waiting and hoping had to stop.

As soon as we got farther out to sea, the dips got deeper, and I had to come into the cockpit to avoid being tossed overboard. Carl had waited for this day to depart so I would have an easy first crossing, with a forecast of six- to eight-foot swells, but the swells were twice that size, and we felt it.

"Get down there and see what's banging around," Carl barked.

I backed down the wooden ladder into the cabin, but my wet hands couldn't hold on tightly enough, and I slipped, hitting my right knee hard on one of the rungs and falling backward onto my butt. I tried to stand, but I stumbled on the slanted floor of the tacking sailboat and fell onto one of the benches that lined its walls.

Beer cans were rolling back and forth as we tacked from left to right, port to starboard. I crawled across the floor, on my aching knee, gathering cans in both arms, to the other side of the boat, where I pulled myself up by a wooden post next to the mini fridge, the source of the problem.

The fridge door hadn't been properly secured. On a port tack, the fridge door closed. On a starboard tack, it opened, letting cans fly. I crammed all the cans back in, but then we tacked back the other direction and the cans flew out again, pelting me on the legs and feet, adding to my burgeoning bruises.

"What the hell are you doing down there?" Carl yelled.

"I'm trying to put these beers away. The fridge fell open," I yelled back. I gave up and crammed the cans in baskets above the benches, resolving to deal with it when we were upright.

After a couple of hours, things calmed down. I was able to sit on the cockpit bench above without holding on for dear life, and I started to enjoy my blue surroundings as the sun dropped lower in the sky.

"There's some dolphins for ya," Carl said.

"Really?" I stood up. "Can I go outside?" Carl had strict safety rules and sometimes required a harness for going out on deck.

He laughed and his eyes softened. "Yeah. Go see 'em."

I put on my inflatable fanny pack and worked my way along the deck as fast as I could while holding tight to the rail. When I got to the bow, I sat down and saw that there was not one but a whole pod of thirty or more dolphins swimming and leaping in our wake.

"Dolphins are a good omen," Carl yelled. I dangled my feet over the bow and felt the waves splash the soles of my feet. I watched their glittering gray backs crest and then disappear to torpedo beneath the turquoise water, emerging on the other side to wiggle-twist in the air. They were performing just for me, it seemed, speaking to me and letting me know it was going to be alright. Carl wasn't spiritual or superstitious, but he believed in the dolphin omen, and so did I.

THE WATCHER

"Your turn." I squinted my eyes to see Carl's skinny legs backing down the ladder, and I looked at the clock: 3 a.m. Carl had done two back-to-back night watches, eight hours of staring into the dark, while I slept on the bench without stirring. I was the worst deckhand ever. All I had done so far was watch dolphins and get a bunch of bruises from beer cans. I tried to lift my shoulders, but I felt like a piece of molten lead.

"I'm getting up," I squeaked.

"It's okay," he said. "The ocean makes you tired." I fell asleep again before I could respond.

The next night, I felt better, stronger, and I was ready to go watch the night with my book, my journal and my bag of chocolates from Gina.

"Don't fall asleep," Carl said.

"I won't." It was only 8 p.m., and I was wide awake. I popped a chocolate in my mouth and waited for my eyes to adjust to the dark.

I felt restless. I stretched my body from one bench to

another to do pushups. I read a few words. I journaled a few words. I looked all around me. Is that a light? Red light means the boat is going away from us, right? Is that an iceberg? Oh God, it's the Titanic. We're going down. I knew this was a mistake. There aren't icebergs in the Caribbean. Is it a whale? It would be sweet to see a whale. I knew this was a good idea. I should meditate. That would be good, I'm going to meditate. With my eyes open. Because I'm watching. Yeah, I'm watching because I'm a sailor and I'm on night watch.

I checked the clock. 8:16.

I never knew how to meditate. I had heard that it consisted of emptying your mind, and that incited in me a big fat laugh, because that was impossible. My mind would never be still, and I assumed anyone whose mind could be still must be simple. I remember asking Juan, "What do you think about all day when you lifeguard?" When he said, "Nothing," I was irritated. "What do you mean 'nothing'? Surely you think of *something*." I couldn't comprehend it.

But that night, as I read *The I Ching*, I learned about a method of meditation that I had not heard of before.

"Observe the flow of your bodily emotions. Do not judge
or resist them; the simple practice of watching them
come, linger, and go without acting on them allows you
to gradually separate them from your thought
processes."[1]

This seemed more doable. I was still allowed to have thoughts. I just had to watch them come and go, like ships in the night. I sat cross-legged on the cushy bench of the cock-

pit, feeling the warm breeze off the Caribbean sea. I closed
my eyes, breathed in through my nose, and I watched.

I am breathing in, I am breathing out.

Did Adam use me?
Did he even care?
Does he think of me?

I am breathing in, I am breathing out.

What if I have an STD?
I don't feel right.
Juan's such a slut that surely I have an STD.

I am breathing in, I am breathing out.

Adam lied to me.
I can't believe he lied to me.
If he lied to his wife, what would stop him from lying
      to me?

I am breathing in, I am breathing out.

What's that sensation?
Maybe an STD.

I am breathing in, I am breathing out.

Maybe it's just a yeast infection.
I have been wearing wet bikinis a lot.

I am breathing in, I am breathing out.

Maybe I should go to the doctor.

Where, though?

How long until we get there?

Will we even make it?

I am breathing in, I am breathing out.

Your intuition said to come on this trip.

But your intuition has been wrong before.

It was wrong about Adam.

Was it wrong about Juan?

If you thought Adam was good and he's bad, could it be
     that you think Juan is bad and he's good?

I am breathing in, I am breathing out. I am breathing in,
I am breathing out.

The timer went off. Whereas in the past, my attempts at
five minutes of meditation seemed interminable, this thirty
minutes passed in a flash. It was striking for me to see,
clearly for the first time, the contents of my mind.

WORRY that Adam used me.

FEAR that Juan infected me.

WORRY that my intuition was wrong.

FEAR that the boat wouldn't make it.

My whole life, I had prided myself on my intelligence
and thought processes, and now that I had become the
watcher of my thoughts, it was evident that the majority of
them were redundant and negative—just WORRY FEAR
WORRY FEAR on repeat. Not a single thought was creativity, hope, happiness or peace.

I looked around me at the endless ocean, and, for the first time, I accepted the silence around me and inside my head. I experienced calm like never before, and I rested my chin on the edge of the cockpit to watch the marine phosphorescence, glowing, glittering and shining in the wake.

---

1. *The I Ching* translation by Brian Browne Walker.

THE BEST REEF

When dawn came, we approached the Guna Yala islands. Carl put me behind the helm, so he could position himself at the bow to drop anchor. It made me nervous, but he said he would call out orders and tell me what to do. I didn't hear instructions but rather, "Shit! Fuck! Godammit!"

The next four hours were a process of "shit, shit" and more "shit." We dragged our anchor all over, back and forth in front of the islands, trying to get it to catch. As I had no real skills or insight to offer in the situation, I prayed.

"I need a drink," Carl said, pouring himself a rum and Coke.

We tried all day, but Carl was getting drunker and the sky was getting darker. If it was fight or flight, I chose flight— the next flight back to Cartagena. But that wasn't an option. Here amidst these remote islands inhabited only by the Guna Yala indigenous people, thirty-six hours of ocean away from Cartagena, I was stranded. I wanted to go home to my

Cartagena comforts, to DeeDee the poodle and Gina's laughter and Juan's warm hugs and kisses. I felt desperate to get out of there, a claustrophobia inside my own body that I suppose is what they describe as cabin fever.

When Carl went back to work, he did finally manage to anchor. Right on top of a reef.

"Ahhhh, fuck!" he yelled. I didn't know the seriousness of getting stuck on a reef, but I was thankful that I wasn't the one driving when it happened.

Carl tried to power off of it. *Rarrrarrarrrarrr* the engine grinded. *Rarrrarrrarrarrr.* We didn't budge.

"The anchor chain must be wrapped around the fucking keel," Carl said.

"What's the keel?" I asked dumbly, as I did with everything that pertained to sailing.

"It's the part on the bottom," Carl answered flatly, as he did with every dumb question I asked.

"What does that mean?"

"It means we're spending the night here. I'm not diving the anchor in the dark." Carl's sad wrinkled eyes cast downward. "I'm going to have another vodka orange juice." He disappeared down the cabin hatch.

I tried to sleep that night, but the boat rocked violently from side to side and made a loud crunching noise as the anchor chain squeezed our hull like a boa constrictor assassinating its prey.

"Is the boat going to be okay?" I yelled up to Carl in the cockpit.

"I'm more worried about the mast," he said. I looked up through my cabin skylight at the tremendous white mast directly overhead.

"When it's your time, it's your time," Carl once said, as he dragged on a cigarette and told me about the young wife and two siblings he lost to lung cancer. It might be your time, Carl, but it's not my time! And yet, despite my fears—despite the swaying and the splintering and the swearing—a day of wind and sea and total exertion let me fall into a deep sleep.

Rarrrararrarrarrrrr. Rarrrarrrarrrarrrarr.

I sat straight up in bed and saw that the sun was rising. The engine grinded as Carl again attempted to motor the boat off the reef, which surely was getting destroyed in the process. I climbed the ladder up to the cockpit.

"You sure sleep a lot," he said. *You sure smoke and drink a lot*, I wanted to say, but I held my tongue.

"Is it still stuck?" I asked.

"I dove the anchor chain this morning and untangled it. Now we just gotta power off this reef."

"You need help?"

"Yeah, get me a beer, will ya?"

That's what Carl needs. More alcohol in his system. I brought him one of the hundreds of Carta Blanca beers that accounted for the bulk of our cargo.

After another hour, Carl finally managed to dislodge us from the reef and set our anchor—in sand this time—about three hundred feet from the tiny Guna Yala island of Korbiski.

I looked around, and a laugh escaped my lips. We were surrounded by pure, turquoise water. There were tiny islands on all sides of us, some packed with straw huts and some with only white sand and palms. A ladder hung over the boat railing behind me.

"I'm going in," I told Carl.

I jumped in with my snorkel gear and went kicking face-down, mesmerized by the clear water and giant starfish, some three feet across. When I finally came up, I was about to collide headfirst into a dugout canoe.

"Hola, buenos días." *Hi, good morning*, I said to the small brown ball of muscle with goggles propped on his forehead. I wasn't sure if he would speak Spanish since I had read that many here only speak Guna.

"Hola." He smiled and went back to his work of cutting conch meat out of shells.

"Soy Erin. ¿Cómo te llamas?" *I'm Erin. What's your name?*

"Soy Abriseño," he said, smiling, returning to his work.

"Perdón. ¿Me puedes decir dónde queda el mejor arrecife?" *Excuse me. Can you tell me where the best reef is?*

"No entiendo tu pregunta," he responded, shrugging, with a sparkle in his smiling almond eyes. *I don't understand your question.* I thought I had said it correctly. How had he not understood? I repeated myself.

"El arrecife. El más bonito." *The reef. The prettiest one.*

He then stood and pointed all around us, 360 degrees. I smiled back, understanding.

We fast-paced North Americans always want to quantify and categorize. We want the "Best Of," the "Top Ten," and we want it fast, because even when we vacation, we do it fast.

We hurry and strive for the so-called "best" moments of our lives, where we are the happiest, most fulfilled, healthiest, most in love. But if we would just stop for a minute, breathe, appreciate the moment for exactly what it is—without judging it as good or bad, worst or best—maybe we could really experience things instead of speeding past them in our desperation to escape toward better.

I believe that Abriseño understood my words, but it was the concept of swimming with your head down, pursuing the "best beauty," while ignoring the beauty all around us, in every moment and every molecule, that eluded him.

Abriseño was right. It was all the best reef.

TENNIS BALLS AND TESTICLES

Carl gave me an assignment of driving the dinghy to the islands to buy him a bottle of rum and a hammock. This was terrifying seeing as my first, and only, lesson on the dinghy had resulted in me almost crashing and destroying a Guna dock made of driftwood.

"I thought you would get it right away," Carl said.

"It's counterintuitive," I said, referring to the fact that if you want to turn starboard, you push the motor toward port, and vice versa.

"Always trust your first instinct," Carl had said. "That's the best one."

"I love how all this sailing wisdom can be applied to life in general."

"Sailing is life," he said. "People have been doing it for thousands of years. Look at the Guna, with their canoes and nothing more than a bed sheet. Sailing is life."

I watched the Guna flying by us, their bed sheets flapping like angel wings, using only the wind's power to move them forward.

Nervous but determined, I crawled down the ladder into the gray rubber dinghy and bailed it out with an empty teriyaki sauce container. Carl loved containers. "That container would make a good bailer," he would say. "We can use this container for your tea." "Don't throw away that container. I have plans for it."

I sat on the edge of the dinghy and clicked the motor down into the water. My heart was pounding. If this were a placid lake, I would have felt alright, but this was the ocean, and the waves were choppy. Not to mention more reef to get caught on. I breathed in deep, put my hand on the throttle and pulled back. *VARRRRRRR!*

"Don't pull back so hard! Just give it a little gas!" Carl yelled at me. "Don't get stuck on a reef! Make sure you tie the knot right!" Thanks for the advice, Carl, and the extra pressure.

I squeezed the handle, white-knuckled, and began crossing, slowly, to the island of Korbiski.

After ten minutes of terror, nearly falling backwards overboard twice, I floated toward the concrete dock, which was farther away than the driftwood dock but couldn't crumble under my incompetence.

My mind raced. Okay. Switch to neutral, but not too soon. Handle up, motor up, click-click, before it scrapes on something. Rope, where's the rope? Crap, where did it go? I ran to the dinghy front and pulled on the rope to find that it had flown out of the dinghy and wrapped itself underneath. Phew. That could have been bad. Right? I'm not sure. I stood and got ready to wrap the rope around one of the concrete posts, provided I could get the knot right.

A shirtless Guna man with a pot belly sauntered down

the dock to watch. He smiled, showing crooked, rotting teeth, and took the rope from me.

"Gracias," I said, exhaling. With his free hand, he helped me climb onto the dock. I looped, swooped and pulled to make the slipknot, which is terribly misnamed, since it really needs to be a no-slip-knot.

I stepped onto the packed dirt of the island, where kids ran by giggling in nothing but cartoon-printed underpants. I walked past a concrete building to my left, where old men sat inside drinking Panamanian Balboa beer at picnic tables, and I continued down a dirt path to the interior of the island.

Though touring boats stopped here sometimes, you wouldn't know it by the way everyone in the village stopped to stare at the gringa walking by in pink shorts, a plaid button-up and low ponytail.

I definitely stood out from the Guna women. They all wore their bright-colored, traditional dress: a patterned wrap skirt, a shirt with poofy sleeves, and a *mola* worn over the waist like a cummerbund. A mola is a square piece of fabric embroidered with tight geometric patterns that look like a maze, forming shapes or sometimes animals. The women all had the same short haircut, floppy on top. Some wore red and yellow bandanas. They wore thick gold nose rings through their septa and thick gold earrings on their stretchy ears. For makeup, they wore only bright fuchsia blush. The men wore jeans and polos, like everywhere else in Latin America.

The dirt path led me to a thatched-roof store, which I entered to find a surprising array of technological devices on display: Samsung Galaxy phones, Canon cameras and SIM cards, which actually kind of worked out here. Sarongs, swim trunks and hammocks hung from the ceiling. Tang, canned tomatoes and other non-perishables lined the back wall.

"Perdón." *Excuse me,* I asked an old man with cataracts, slumped over in a chair against the wall. He snortled awake.

"Hmf, ¿qué quieres?" *What do you want?*

"¿Cuánto valen las hamacas?" *How much are your hammocks?*

I heard giggling behind me. I turned around to see four little girls who had followed me into the store and huddled by the doorway. They hunched their shoulders and pushed one another.

"Tú eres guapa," one said. *You're pretty.*

"¡Ustedes son las guapas!" *You guys are the pretty ones!*

They giggled again, and a girl with shoulder-length hair neatly held by a headband pointed at her shorter friend with fuzzy, messy hair tucked behind large ears.

"Ella no cree que se ve guapa." *She doesn't think she's pretty.*

"What?" I said, in Spanish. "You don't know how beautiful you are? With those beautiful high cheek bones and almond eyes?"

It hurt my heart, to think that these eight-year-old girls, with their perfect brown skin and broad noses, could not see that they were beautiful. Here on an island, miles away from media and fashion magazines, our cultures shared a lack of confidence. The messy-haired girl, called Claritza, grabbed me by the hand.

"Come to my house."

"You need to ask permission," I said, uncertain whether

the traditional Guna wanted me traipsing around their village let alone their homes. Sweet little Claritza looked at me as though I had two heads.

"From your parents. Ask permission from your parents?"

"No," she laughed. "You're just coming to my house."

I looked to the old man, now standing behind the counter watching. He smiled, the wrinkles beneath his eyes consuming them like sand around stone. Just as the Gunas had no concept of seeking out the best reef, I would soon see that they also had no sense of *my* house or *my* anything for that matter.

The girls grabbed my hands and led me behind the store, farther down the path past Guna huts. A few of the huts had painted wood signs reading panadería, *bakery*, and one was labeled "Iglesia Palabra de Vida," *Word of Life Church.*

As we walked, I looked in the doorless huts at families bathing naked babies, lying in hammocks and cooking over two-burner gas stoves.

Fluorescent yellow tennis balls lay all over the ground, and Nilka, the girl in the headband, picked one up.

"My little brother just got his," she said, picking one up and rotating it to show me his name written in Sharpie on the side. At about two years old, she explained, every kid on the island received a tennis ball, and that was his or her single toy. They bounced them between one another, invented games, and appeared to be truly happy with the one item and their imaginations to entertain them.

You would think that, since they only had the one thing, they would guard them possessively and hide them away under their mattresses (if they had mattresses). Instead, they rolled them all over the island, between huts and between friends, never once uttering "mine." They came and went among one another's doorless huts, sharing food, sharing resources, sharing all.

"This is my sister," said Claritza, pointing to a twenty-something Queen Bee with a full belly hanging out the bottom of her tank top and spilling over the top of purple spandex shorts.

With a smart phone wedged between her bosom, she sat in a plastic chair and groomed herself with a plastic comb in a handheld mirror. She looked up for a second to acknowledge me, her eyes dull and frowning.

Other teen girls sat around her in plastic chairs preening, adjusting the plastic clips in their hair and pulling at their tops and shorts. I eyed them, wondering which one made precious Claritza think she wasn't pretty.

All of the younger kids in diapers and their cartoon underpants toddled around us. They were covered in what looked like brown age spots.

"¿Qué tienen?" *What do they have?* I asked.

"Varicela," said the Queen Bee. That didn't sound good. I didn't know the translation for varicela, but I hoped it meant chicken pox, as one of the toddlers scratched his belly and grabbed my hand.

"Do you girls know where I can get a good hammock?" I asked.

Queen Bee jumped up and ran to their dugout canoe, parked behind her on the trash side of the island. From a distance, it all looked so pristine, but when you got close, when you crossed to the untoured side of the island, it was beer cans, dirty diapers, broken rubber flip-flops, pieces of plastic and chunks of Styrofoam, all piled high and gradually eroding into the ocean.

"Where's she going?" I asked Claritza.

"We're going to Wichuabuala. Can I ride with you?" she pulled on my arm and begged. I wanted to take her, I really did, but my dinghy experiences had been less than expert, and I didn't want to be known as the gringa who killed a Guna.

"Me too. Can I go with you?" Nilka grabbed my other arm.

"I can fit one," I said. At least I could limit my manslaughter charge to one Guna and not two.

"Me!" Nilka claimed the spot that Claritza asked for first, but Claritza, as unselfish with boat rides as with tennis balls, didn't contest it and ran to jump in the canoe with Queen Bee.

I lifted Nilka under her arms and lowered her awkwardly down into the dinghy, almost tumbling over the top of her. I felt that chest-pounding anxiety again as I untied my rope.

"Sit down here and hold onto that handle, tight," I told her. I putted toward the neighboring island at a snail's pace, as Nilka watched me with a smile but also a hint of disappointment. She probably thought the fancy motored dinghy was going to take us flying, the wind in her hair and ocean spray on her lips.

The dugout canoe beat us there, where the girls climbed onto the dock like agile ninjas. I laughed at my attempts to "help" sweet obliging Nilka into the dinghy. She probably could get in and out of a boat like a ninja, too. She probably knew every inch of the reef and could tie a no-slip-knot with her eyes closed.

The girls helped me buy Carl's rum and hammock at a fair price, and I bought them all Uvas, grape sodas, the cans from which would be thrown onto the trash heap. I helped them load a big box of freshly baked bread into their canoe, and I waved goodbye to them as they paddled away.

"Eres bella." *You're beautiful*, I reminded Claritza.

She touched her shoulder to her cheek giggling and waved as they glided home.

I strolled the dirt path back to the dock and, not ready to resume doing nothing on the boat with Carl, I peeked inside a doorless concrete building.

"Is this a restaurant?" I asked the tiny woman inside.

"Yes."

"What do you have?"

She pointed at crates full of rotting vegetables on the floor and opened the lid to a freezer box to reveal stacks of red and gold cans of cold Balboa beer. Supplies here were akin to those on Carl's boat.

"I'll have a beer," I said, handing my $1.50 to the sulking teenage boy sitting at the register.

The one-room, dirt-floor restaurant consisted of two long picnic tables. I chose to sit diagonally across from the one other customer, an old man with a baseball cap and a cross hanging around his neck.

The man, Pascual, and I started talking, and by the time I finished my beer, it must have been Guna quitting time, because the whole place had filled with Guna men ordering a beer for every hand.

"Let us get you another," Pascual said, waving his hand at the attending Guna woman.

"Where are the other women?" I asked, noticing that the fifteen or so other patrons were all men.

"Women aren't allowed to drink on this island," Pascual said.

"But I'm a woman, and I'm drinking."

"Yes, but you do not live here, so it's okay," he explained. The Guna woman served me my beer, and I looked at her lined, tired face.

According to the guidebooks, the Guna Yala Indian culture is a matriarchal society, meaning that the women were the heads of household and controlled the family's finances and important decisions.

"I read that women make the decisions." I tentatively broached the topic with Alberto, a sixty-something man with piercing light blue eyes and an excitement for explaining his culture.

"The *selas* make the decisions," he said. "I'm a sela." He patted his chest proudly. "We decide on the rules and regulations of the island."

"Are any of the selas women?" I asked.

"No, no. The selas are all men."

My brow furrowed in confusion. I wished I could ask the women how they felt about these rules, but they all seemed too busy working.

At that moment, a short, snaggle-toothed man stood and started hopping around like a little bird, theatrically telling a story I didn't understand, since it was a mix of Guna and Spanish.

"His testicles got bitten off by a shark," Alberto translated to Spanish.

"There are sharks here?"

"No, don't worry dear. The sharks are not close to the islands. They are farther out. This man was diving very far from here."

The performing man hopped up to me and got close to my face.

"My testicles got bit off," he said, in Spanish. "Do you want to see?" He hop-turned around and bent over, about to drop his pants. I covered my eyes with both hands and squealed.

"No! No, I believe you." I kept my hands over my eyes, and they all laughed at the man's antics, at their ability to horrify a gringa.

"It's okay. You can uncover your eyes now," Alberto said.

I peeked, and, seeing that the man had staggered back to his bench, I dropped my hands. Seeing that every man around me was getting progressively drunker, I decided to make my exit.

"Well gentlemen, thank you for the beers. I really should be getting back to the boat."

"Please stay!" One of the younger men with rudimentary tattoos that looked like children's doodles stood up and pleaded. "Let us buy you one more."

I may normally have been dumb enough to give in to this request, always sacrificing safety for adventure, but I had to face the daunting drive back across the choppy waves, and it didn't seem like a good idea to undertake it half drunk.

"I'd love to, but the captain will be mad with me if I don't get back soon. Thank you so much, though. I really appreciate you all teaching me about your culture."

They had taught me a lot over the past couple of hours, everything from how they use the *baba*, sea snail slime, to make a lather for washing their hands to how coconuts are a commodity for which there are a strict set of rules.

"Any time," Alberto said, clasping my hand between his two rough, wrinkled hands.

Alberto walked me out to the dock and helped me down into the dinghy. He untied my thank-God-it-didn't-slip-knot and, as I floated away backward, those intense blue eyes looked like they might cry.

"Te quiero," he said. *I love you.*

CAPTAIN INCOMPETENT

After a week sitting off the coast of Korbiski, we pulled up our hard-earned anchor hold and headed for another Guna Yala island called Chicheme.

I was excited, because lots of tourism boats loaded with backpackers stopped there to swim and play, so I might be able to make some friends who didn't try to show me their testicles.

Carl had me steer while he barked confusing, conflicting orders at me and drank his rum and Coke out of a seahorse mug.

"Port! Go toward port."

I steered toward port, though the navigation software showed a starboard course and it appeared we were heading straight for the shallow reef surrounding another island. He was the expert, I figured, since he told me he had been sailing for ten years.

"What the fuck are you doing?" Carl screamed.

"I was going toward port."

"Well fuck, Erin, you know I'm dyslexic," he said, taking another drink.

My eyes widened and I pressed my lips together, changing our course toward starboard.

As we got closer, we both started checking the scene out with binoculars. We counted at least twelve sailboats in the Bay of Chicheme, and I was getting antsy. People! Civilization!

Carl spread out a map showing the varying ocean depths at the entry to the bay so we could see where the best point of access was.

"The guidebook says we need to enter to the left of the small island with the single palm tree," I said. "The right side is too shallow."

"I know that. I read it, too," Carl said, annoyed.

The two-hour crossing felt slow, but now we were coming up on that single-palm island fast. I steered us toward port.

"What are you doing?" Carl yelled. "We have to go around the other side. Starboard! Starboard!"

I thought maybe I misunderstood the maps. And maybe I had misunderstood the words in the guidebook:

"Enter the Bay of Chicheme to the left of the island with
the single palm tree."

At any rate, I wasn't going to crash the boat and have it be my fault, so I listened to Captain Carl. He ran to the bow and looked over the edge to advise me on the reef.

"Port! Port!" he yelled back. "Fuck! Godammit."

We would crash right into the reef and the single-palm island if we went directly port, so I pulled hard toward starboard and took us in a circle so that we could do the approach all over again, this time entering "to the left of the island with the single palm tree."

Carl took over the helm, which I was glad for, so I could at least heave myself overboard the next time he did something crazy.

For our next attempt, we were coming in hot, way too fast amidst the many boats. People stood on their decks watching, looking fearful.

"Erin, take over," Carl said. "I gotta drop anchor." We had to physically drop and crank up the anchor, because the electronic wench was broken, and Carl refused to fix it until we got to cheaper Guatemala.

My chest thumped, but I took the helm and held our course straight as he went out to the bow, bent his little wrinkly body over and heaved the anchor with its thick chain into the water.

"Reverse!" he yelled, "Put 'er in reverse!"

I did as told, but the anchor didn't catch and we were drifting starboard toward another sailboat. Carl came back to the cockpit and grabbed the helm again, and I stepped back, terrified, looking all around for answers, because apparently Captain Carl had none.

Two men who had been watching us from their deck came speeding up to us on a dinghy, the bronzed one's chest glistening and shoulder-length, sun-lightened hair blowing in the wind.

"¿Hablan francés?" *Do you speak French?* asked a shorter, pudgier one with curly brown hair.

"Si, el capitán habla francés." *Yes, the captain speaks French*, I told him, since Carl had told me that he grew up in Montreal and French was his first language.

The men tied on their dinghy, climbed aboard and addressed Carl in French. Carl muttered back a few inept words that even I could tell were wrong.

"Él no habla francés," *He doesn't speak French,* said Pello, the short one, in Spanish.

"Yo traduciré," I said. *I'll interpret.* I also tried to interpret in my own mind why Carl didn't know shit about sailing or speaking French.

Pello took the wheel and steered us away from danger, while the bronze boy, a Spaniard named Javier, pulled up the anchor with his bulging muscles. I stayed by his side, leaning against the rail and posing in my coral-colored bikini and cutoff jean shorts. You know, in case I had to translate. We spoke in Spanish, so Carl couldn't understand.

"How long have you been traveling with this guy?" Javier asked.

"A little more than a week. I've never sailed before, so I have no idea what I'm doing."

"Neither does he."

"But he said he's had this boat ten years. He said he's done the Caribbean circuit several times."

"Ha, I don't think so."

I raised my eyebrows and widened my eyes. "Well, shit."

I walked back to the cockpit, where Pello and Carl were struggling to communicate with one another, so I could translate. But I didn't translate everything.

"Da miedo. Da miedo," Pello kept repeating, eyes wide. *It's frightful. It's frightful.* "Este hombre no sabe lo que está haciendo." *This guy doesn't know what he is doing.*

"What can we do? Is there somewhere we can anchor here?" I asked.

"We can try," Pello said, "But the wind is really strong

here in the bay, and I don't think you have enough anchor chain to hold you. Not to mention that this dumb thing will catch the wind even more," he said, gesturing toward the plastic enclosure around the cockpit. "You would drift right into one of the other boats."

Pello and Javier tried their best to set our inadequate anchor in the bay, but they couldn't do it and steered us around to the other side of the island where the winds weren't as strong.

I relaxed knowing we were in the strong, able hands of sailors who really knew what they were doing. They put us in a good spot, and Javier even put on goggles and dove the anchor to make extra sure it wasn't going anywhere.

Carl offered the guys some rum and Cokes, which I mixed and brought to them on the deck.

"Thank you, guys," Carl said. "I guess I'm just an old marina hound. I'm always docked at marinas, so I haven't had to anchor too much."

Javier and I flirted, but when Pello was ready for dinner, they left on their dinghy, and I was left alone with Captain Incompetent. Captain Liar. Captain Doesn't-Speak-French. Captain Doesn't-Know-How-To-Anchor. Captain Rum-and-Coke. I stayed out on the deck a long time, until it got dark, looking out at a sailboat lying on its side, beached on the reef in the distance.

SWAMP THING STOWAWAY

"Hey, look who our new neighbors are," Carl said, handing me the binoculars. Nosy Carl loved commenting on incoming boats and their passengers.

"The Black Dragon!" It was Bjorn and Emily, the young couple who were docked next to us at the marina in Cartagena.

"Maybe I can buy some dollars from them," Carl said. "I have all these fucking Colombian pesos." As with our fresh water supply, Carl had not adequately planned for the amount of dollars he would need in the islands, having borrowed about one hundred from me thus far.

"I'll go!" I volunteered, not concerned about money but excited to talk to people, real live people whom I knew and trusted.

I motored the dinghy over to the pirate-style boat, with black painted wood and intricate carved dragons, and I asked permission to come aboard.

"Come on up!" Emily said, surprisingly put together for a sailor girl, with her red lipstick on full round lips and cat-eye eyeliner highlighting amber eyes. "You want a coffee?"

"That'd be great," I said, sitting on a cushioned bench on the stylish wooden deck.

She descended into the cabin and came back with a big mug of coffee with cream and sugar, a real luxury. She sat on the bench across from me, leaned on her hand, looked me in the eyes and asked, "How are things going?"

She gave me the opening I needed. I began to pour out the tales of all our complications, from being stuck on a reef to needing outsider help to accomplish a solid anchor off the coast of Chicheme, where we had been now for more than a week. I felt like a crime scene victim, huddled there with my coffee, with Bjorn and Emily looking on, eyes arched in worry. Bjorn propped a muscled, blonde-haired leg on the bench.

"I was worried about you, seeing you getting on the boat with him," he said in his strong Norwegian accent, which made everything sound more grave. "I was going to say something, but I didn't want to interfere. I thought maybe you knew him, that he was your uncle or something."

"No, just a guy my friends introduced me to," I said. Hearing it out loud made my stupidity more evident.

"Does the guy drink every day?" Bjorn asked.

"Yeah, he does, but he never seems drunk."

"That is because he is always drunk," Bjorn said. There was that gravity again. I thought about a conversation Megan and I had before we left.

"I worry about Carl," she had said.

"What do you mean?"

"He just sits there all day drinking and smoking. I think he needs to get back out at sea, get moving again."

I nodded. I wanted him to be well, then and now. I wanted to be company for Carl, the family he no longer had, after losing his wife, his parents, his siblings. I felt a sadness and affection for him, and I didn't want to leave him alone, dangerous though he may be.

Emily touched my knee. "Listen. I'm gonna tell you what you're gonna do. Get a boat to port and from there, get yourself to Panama City. From there, you can fly to Fort Lauderdale and, a cute young girl like you, you can get hired on a superyacht where you'll make good money, where you'll be *safe*." She made eye contact and squeezed my knee. "The ocean is not to be taken lightly. Run. Run fast and run now."

———

"What movie you want to watch tonight?" Carl asked, showing me the options, which were always gladiator epics with lots of blood or action flicks with lots of explosions. I chose the one with the hunkiest actor, and we each settled onto our respective benches in the cockpit.

"Want half my Hershey bar?" Carl offered.

"No thanks," I chirped back. I had already eaten five times what Carl had that day. "I'm going to stick to crackers."

"You want peanut butter and jam for them?"

"Yes!" I felt six years old. Carl was the drunken sailor grandpa I never had.

When Carl went to bed around eight, I wrote, sitting cross-legged on the bench, looking out at the ocean.

The breeze swirled loose hairs to tickle my neck, and I listened to the wind-energy spinner whir and whistle. The boat creaked with each side-to-side motion. I didn't realize how much we swayed until I saw it from the island one night, our little blue light ping-ponging back and forth. We swayed, like a bassinet, and my mind and body had adjusted to believe we were solid, upright. How many other things had I mistaken as solid when they were in sway?

For the first time, I was learning to be okay as just me, alone. Ever since I was twelve, I always sought out an accompaniment, a boy, to make me feel whole. Finally, at twenty-nine years old, I stopped scouting the horizon for something more, because all that was on the horizon was ocean. I could stop searching and just be.

Phtthoooohhh. I heard a breathy exhale and hurried onto the deck.

A single dolphin circled our boat, the full moon reflecting off her shiny, silvery back. She surfaced to exhale, and I sat on the aft bench, watching her.

I had felt afraid after my conversation with Emily, but the dolphin's breath comforted me. It was the dolphin omen, back again, to tell me everything was going to be okay. Her breath, for me, was God's breath, unseen but heard deep within my heart saying, "Stay." Though you're bored and bruised and Carl is a semi-crazy and semi-competent sailor, "Stay," she breathed. "Stay."

"Carl you son-of-a-bitch!" A bulb-nosed, crater-faced man with a ponytail floated up to our boat in a dinghy.

Carl got up from his bench to look over the edge. "Hi, Axel," he said, unenthused.

"Tie us off, you bastard!" Axel's dinghy bumped up against our port side.

I stepped onto the deck, and he threw me a rope to wrap around the cleat.

"It's been a long time." Axel said, his voice raw and screaming.

"Yeah," Carl said, sounding like he wished it could have been longer.

Axel climbed onto the deck. "Hello," he said, holding out his hand. I went to shake it, and he lifted and kissed my hand, eyeing me with bulging eyes above a veiny nose. "Carl, how'd you get a pretty girl like this to sail with you, you miserable bastard?"

"She works for me, Axel."

"Lucky man. You can work for us, sweetheart. I'll pay you better than this cheap bastard."

"What do you want?" Carl asked.

"Do you have a pliers?" he asked in his almost-right English. "Our fucking anchor is broke, piece of shit boat, and we don't have nothing to fix it."

"Erin, go get Axel some pliers from the toolbox," Carl said.

I brought back pliers, hoping they would ply this weirdo to go away. I looked into the dinghy, at Axel's cohort, a handsome man about my age with a full head of black hair. He could stay.

"I'm Ethan," he said, finally speaking up and revealing he was North American.

"Hey, Ethan. Where you from?"

"New York. How about you? Your English is good."

"That's because I'm from Oregon." I had gotten extra tan from sailing, so people were assuming I was Latina more than ever.

"Wow. What brought you all the way down here?" he asked.

"I could ask you the same."

"I came down here on vacation, and I wanted to stay longer, so I got a job cooking on Axel's boat. I'm a chef."

"Nice. You guys are probably eating better than we are, with my crappy cooking."

"Erin's a good cook," Carl said, complimenting the food he never ate, most of it thrown overboard.

"We have to go," Axel interrupted, annoyed that quiet Ethan was getting attention. "We gotta fix this fucking anchor. You guys should come over and have some lunch."

"Sounds great!" I said.

After they motored away, Carl told me the story of how he knew Axel the Argentinian.

"The guy's a swindler. I hired Axel to work for me two years ago when I was sailing in the ABC islands. We sailed around for a few weeks, and when we got to the marina in Aruba, he had nowhere to go. So I said I'd let him stay on the boat 'til he figured out what to do, but he never left. And he was filthy. That's why I hire women now. Men are filthy. I told him after six weeks he had to go, and he made a big scene of it."

"Wow, that's crazy," I said. "Why is he a swindler? Did he steal from you?"

"I gave him my Skype log-in so he could call his girl-friend when he was on the boat with me. A year after he left, he was still using it and charging more minutes to my credit card."

"Couldn't you just change your password?"

"I don't know, Erin," he said, disappearing down the

hatch, irritated that I had missed the point that Axel is a terrible person.

While Carl was napping the next day, another dinghy came to the boat.

"Hey there, neighbor," said the sixty-something bald man who approached.

"Hi."

"You the owner of this boat?"

"No, I'm just the deckhand. You need to talk to the captain?"

"Nah, it's alright. I saw you guys come into the bay last week, and it looked like this boat was having trouble steering. You might want to check your rudder, because in this salty water it gets gunked up real fast and that might be why you're having problems."

"Thank you. I'll tell the captain." When Carl woke up, I delivered the message.

"That's a bunch of bullshit," he said, cracking a beer. "I had that rudder scraped when we were in Carta-haynya."

"Oh. Okay," I said.

I started to worry that, after now three warnings (four if you count the reef), that I wasn't so safe with Captain Carl, dolphin omen or not. I swam the quarter mile to the island to meditate, to see if the universe had any answers. With an hour of meditation delivering no clear feeling one way or the other, I decided to stay.

As I stood on the beach, stretching my arms and getting ready for my swim back, Axel and Ethan emerged from the tropical foliage to untie their dinghy from a palm log.

"You're going to swim?" Ethan asked.

"Yeah. I like the exercise, and I don't like to strand Carl without the dinghy, in case he wants to go somewhere."

"Come on, we'll take you back," Axel offered. We motored away from the shore toward Carl's boat.

"Do you want to come over for lunch?" Ethan asked.

"Sure," I said, and he steered us starboard toward their rusty little boat, which was anchored one hundred feet from our own.

Ethan assembled big sub sandwiches while Axel talked.

"So how is it you have come to sail with Carl?" Axel asked.

"Some friends of mine knew him, and he needed help, so I went."

"Well, be careful."

"What do you mean?"

"I like Carl and all, but man, I'm telling you, Carl don't know shit."

"I thought he's been sailing for ten years."

"He told you that? Carl started sailing when he hired me two years ago. That was when he got that boat. And he don't know shit."

Ethan handed me my sub sandwich, and I took a bite and chewed, staring at the ground while Axel kept talking.

"And he's fucking crazy, man. I was on there with him and his fucking girlfriend, and they was always fucking fighting and shit, throwing shit and screaming."

"I can't imagine that," I said. "Carl curses a lot, but I've never seen him like that."

"Oh yeah, man, he fucking strangled her this one time."

"He strangled her?"

"Yeah man, he fucking strangled her."

Ethan leaned against the counter and crossed his arms, looking at me with concern. I took another bite of my sandwich.

I didn't tell Carl that I was terrified of his sailing skills and alleged strangulation. Rather, that evening I told him that sailing wasn't for me, that I missed my friends and life on land in Cartagena. He understood but insisted that I stay with him for another couple of weeks, until we got to Bocas del Toro, Panama. He rightly advised it would be much cheaper and easier to get back to Cartagena from there. After Carl went to sleep that night, around 8 p.m., I got out the sailing guidebook to check out the crossing to come. I'm paraphrasing, but it said something like:

> "The approach to Bocas del Toro is dangerous, even for the most experienced sailor."

Upon reading this bit of advice, I literally flung myself overboard and swam the hundred feet of dark ocean to a catamaran anchored nearby. The group of laughing, dining backpackers looked with horror at the swamp monster that emerged from the dark water and crawled onto their boat's aft deck.

"Is the captain here?" I wheezed between sucking air. They stared, silent.

When I stepped forward into the light and showed that I was not Swamp Thing but a young woman, they relaxed and carried on drinking, unconcerned. The middle-aged captain came out of the cabin and addressed me in Spanish.

"Qué necesitas?" *What do you need?*

I spilled the past month's events erratically. "I need to get to shore. I'm a deckhand for that captain over there and he nearly killed us. He got us stuck on a reef and he's always drunk. He doesn't know how to anchor. He nearly ran us into several boats. He strangled his ex-girlfriend. He has my passport in his safe. Please."

He blinked, expressionless and unimpressed by my desperate plea for my life. "These tourists paid a lot of money to take this boat, and it's already crowded," he said. "Let me ask the others if they would mind you coming along."

Thankfully, they agreed to let me be their Swamp Thing stowaway. The following morning, I packed my things, said goodbye to Carl, and rode with them to "port," a muddy shoreline on the outskirts of dense Panamanian jungle. I crammed into a four-wheel drive Jeep with the backpackers and caught a ride to Panama City, where I could find a flight back to my beloved Cartagena and all its comforts.

ESTOY EN CARTAGENA CONTIGO

A swim, a dinghy, a catamaran, a Jeep, a week in Panama City, a taxi and a plane later, I was back to comfortable Cartagena.

Seeing Juan's big white smile at the airport was the greatest sight, and I dropped my backpack to run to him. He picked me up and we kissed a long time, sometimes stopping for air or to laugh and look one another up and down.

"You look beautiful," he said.

"Thank you. You look so handsome." He looked the most handsome I'd ever seen him, with his hair cut the way I liked it, short on the sides, and a fresh white t-shirt emphasizing his broad shoulders and strong chest.

He carried my bag and bought me a lemonade. We walked straight from the airport to Berlinas bus company, holding hands, and we hopped in a van headed for the neighboring city of Barranquilla, to see his family.

I said all my *mucho-gustos* to his mom, his three brothers, and several boarders living in his mom's house, then Juan and I made for his bedroom.

Once inside the tiny closet of a room alone, we faced one another and smiled. He grabbed me, squeezed me close, and held my head to his chest. He thought he wasn't going to see me for a year, and I had called him the day before my flight to tell him I was coming back.

I hadn't missed him on the boat, but this, right now, felt good. We stripped off our clothes and held one another, despite the heat, as I told him what had happened to me on the boat.

"¿Recuerdas la primera escritura que hicimos?" I asked. *Do you remember the first writing that we did?*

"Sí," he said.

"¿El que dijo que no estuve aquí? ¿Que no sabía como cruzar la distancia?" *The one that said I wasn't here? That I didn't know how to cross the distance?*

Juan looked me in the eyes, and we connected, really this time.

"¿Ahora estás aquí?" *Now you're here?*

"Sí. Estoy en Cartagena contigo." *Yes. I'm in Cartagena with you.*

'Estoy en Cartagena' had the exact same cadence as 'Estoy enamorada,' *I'm in love.*

Juan pulled me in tighter and wrapped his arms and legs around me, kissing my cheek and neck. I let him hold me so long, longer than I had let anyone hold me before, until we fell asleep in each other's arms.

THE CRACK HOUSE

After a few days visiting his family, Juan and I walked the glorious alleys of Cartagena, together again, searching for an apartment where he could stay the night without having to hide in the closet and pee in bottles. We were laughing, stealing kisses, holding hands, when I heard a familiar voice.

"Erin."

I looked across the street, and I had to blink my eyes a few times to process the skinny figure with a scraggly beard and long hair piled in a man-bun.

"Elías." I dropped Juan's hand. "¿Qué haces aquí?" *What are you doing here?*

"I came to find you." He said exactly what I feared. Elías, sweet Elías who had nursed my ailing soul in Peru, had backpacked 2,925 miles over land with less than one hundred dollars in his pocket, to come see me. Juan Calderón, a head taller than Elías, stood behind me, arms crossed.

"This is Juan," I said, leaving it at that. I gave Elías a big hug. "How long will you be here?"

"I don't know. A little while."

"Let's catch up soon," I said, giving him my Colombian phone number. "It's good to see you."

Juan and I walked away, not holding hands. "Who was that?"

"That's Elías. I've told you about him."

"Your ex-boyfriend?"

"Kind of. We were more friends."

"I like his teeth," Juan said cruelly, referring to the big gap, not perfect like his own.

"I loved Elías for his soul," I retorted. "You can fix teeth. You can't fix an ugly soul." Juan shut up, and I excused his mean-spirited comments as being fueled by jealousy.

By the end of the day, after searching everywhere from Laguito to Marbella, we found me a place in the city center that was twenty-five dollars more than Beni's place, with none of the amenities. Gina called it The Crack House.

We entered through an oil-stained, wrought iron gate guarded by two ancient men sleeping in plastic chairs, heads back and mouths open to display few wiggly teeth.

Inside the gate, the "lobby" had a low ceiling with thick bundles of exposed wires running along the tops of the walls. It reeked of urine, and smashed cockroaches littered the rough concrete floor.

We climbed four stories up broken-tile stairs, trying to interpret the cryptic black graffiti on the poo-smudged, yellow walls. At the end of the hall, on the fourth floor, through another padlocked gate, was my new home: a ten-by-ten-foot concrete room with a sagging twin bed and a forest green love seat. It had its own tiny bathroom, an ant-farm of a filthy kitchen that we shared with the neighbor, and, the kicker, an independent entry so Juan could come and go as he pleased.

It was basic, but after a good scrub, some fresh Caribbean-colored sheets and a turquoise bathmat, it was cozy enough for Juan and me to snuggle into.

DON'T GIVE IT TO JUST ANYONE

After a week of nonstop Juan, staying over every night, I needed some girl time. I went out for an evening ice cream with Gina, and Juan went out with Omar, his pretentious lawyer friend who spoke condescendingly to everyone and cheated on his girlfriend every chance he got. (He wasn't my favorite.)

When I got home from my girl date, Juan wasn't there, so I tried to call him, feeling uneasy. I called and called until finally, at 10 p.m., he picked up. He said he'd be back "más tardecito," *a little bit later*, which I had learned could mean anything from ten minutes to ten hours.

At 11 p.m., I lay in bed worrying when my phone rang. I scrambled to find it in my balled-up sheets, relieved that Juan was checking in. It was Elías.

"You want to meet in Plaza Trinidad? I'm here playing soccer."

"Maybe." I looked at the clock. "Sure." I decided that if I went out, it would help the time and worrying pass faster. I tried calling Juan but, as usual, he didn't answer. I left the apartment, and I didn't leave a key.

I got to the plaza, and Elías smiled, lighting up. He came to give me a hug. "Will you hold these?" he asked, pulling some change and bits of paper from his sweatpants pocket.

"Sure." I smiled. Elías was easy to trust.

He was good at soccer and great with kids, and I smiled as I watched him play and interact. While we weren't compatible as lovers, I would always feel love for him and his beautiful soul.

Upon finishing the game, he came back to where I was sitting. "You want to go for a walk?"

"No, not really," I said, worrying that it would give the wrong appearance if we ran into Juan.

Elías's golden face looked sad, a way I never wanted to make him feel. "Well, okay. Just for a bit," I said.

We walked out of Getsemaní, past the clock tower, and we stopped at the tourist dock across from the Convention Center.

"Are you okay?" He could sense my discord.

I started crying, without prior warning or desire. He put his arm around me and leaned around to see my face. "It's just..." I sobbed. "I don't know what I'm doing. Everything I write is shit. I'm trying to write a book, but I've hardly got anything. All these months and nothing." Something about Elías's spirit made me open up wide and share the things I couldn't say to anyone else.

"Hey." He wiped a tear with his index finger and faced me, grabbing both arms. "Nothing you write will ever be shit."

"You haven't even read my stuff."

"I know, but I know you, and I know that nothing you write could ever possibly be shit."

I cried harder and he hugged me. I had shared more emotion with him, in those fifteen minutes walking, than I had with Juan ever. We sat down on the dock, dangling our feet over the water.

"How did you make it here?" I asked.

"Gonzalo and I played music on the street to get money. He played guitar and I played my djembe."

"I'm impressed. That made you enough?"

"We don't eat much." Elías had been skinny before, but now he was emaciated.

"Elías! You need to eat."

"We stand outside restaurants sometimes and ask for leftovers, anything they might throw away."

I laughed. "Remember when we ate those people's left-over pizza? Brendan looked at us like we were savages."

"We were such niños," he said, laughing. Elías and I were like kids together, playing on playgrounds, sitting on the ground eating ice cream, dancing in the rain.

"I liked it."

"Me too," he said, touching my hand. "Erin, I want to tell you two things."

"Okay."

"First. Please don't write about me."

"I can't promise that."

At this, Elías got up and stormed off. "The second doesn't matter anymore."

Elías was not the first or the last person in my life to ask me not to write about them. It is a risk you take, when dating a writer, and one you should understand well. We can't help but write about the people who impact our hearts. It's like asking a rooster not to crow at the sun, a wolf not to howl at the moon. It's what we were made to do. If you want to be excluded from our musings, be mediocre. But Elías was anything but mediocre. He was the sun and the moon.[1]

"Elías." I chased after him and touched him on the shoulder. "I care about you. I pray for you."

"Pray, ha." He shrugged me off. "A lot of good that does."

"I know you don't believe in it, but I do. And maybe that should mean something."

"See you around," he said, and I began to cry again.

Ever tender-hearted, Elías turned around and hugged me as I cried on his shoulder for the thousandth time. "I'm sorry, Erin. I'm sorry. Please. Let me walk you home."

Elías walked with me back to The Crack House. Now 12:30 a.m., Juan still wasn't there. Elías didn't know Juan lived with me or that he hadn't come home that night, but maybe he had an idea.

"Erin, I'm going to tell you the other thing, the second thing I wanted to say."

"Yes. Please."

"Cuida tu corazón. No lo entregues a cualquiera." *Take care of your heart. Don't give it to just anyone.*

I hugged him tight. "Thank you, Elías. I needed that."

I went to bed but couldn't sleep, as I watched the little tinted window above the door, waiting for Juan's tap-tap to be let in. By the time 2 a.m. rolled around, I started to wish he wouldn't come. My heart felt heavy and my chest tight.

"I'm afraid of being alone," I said, out loud.

I heard a stronger voice, inside of me: "You'll never be alone." This voice—which wasn't really an audible voice but a deep Knowing—is something I had started to feel ever since the day I prayed for a solution to my marriage to John.

The Knowing was calmer, wiser, uninfluenced by ego or fear. *The I Ching* refers to it as the Higher Self, and that's how I think of it also. It is the self that is more tuned into the divine than the world, a self that knows it is protected, loved and forever connected.

At that moment, I heard the tap. The lights were out. I could pretend to be asleep. My intuition said be still, but my ego wanted his love and affection, so I got up, turned on the light and unlocked the door.

"Hey baby," he said, leaning in to give me a kiss.

"You were out late," I said.

"Yeah, you know, I was with Omar and he kept wanting to drink more."

"What did you guys do tonight?"

"We hung out in the Plaza Trinidad, drinking some wine and some stuffs."

"Some stuff." I corrected him. "I was in Plaza Trinidad. I didn't see you there."

"I didn't see you there, either." He narrowed his eyes. "Were you with Gina?"

"I was earlier. Then I came home, and you weren't here and you didn't answer your phone, so I went to meet Elías."

"You hung out with Elías?"

"He invited me to the plaza to watch him play soccer. I was bored waiting for you, so I went."

"Elías your ex-boyfriend?"

"Yeah, and now he's my friend."

"Yeah, well, I trust you." The way he said 'I trust you' sounded like the contrary. "I'm going to take a shower." Juan never wanted to shower at night. He usually just stripped off his clothes and crawled sweatily into bed.

"Are you sure you were in the plaza?" I accused.

He put his hands on his hips and cocked his head.

"Never mind," I said. "I trust you." My 'I trust you' sounded much like his. I crawled into bed and faced the wall.

After he got out of the shower, he sat on the side of the bed and touched my hot back with his cool wet hand. "Baby, I'm sorry. I do trust you." I rolled over, and he could see that I was crying. He laid down and pulled me in close.

The next day, I told Juan I needed space, but what I really needed was to take care of my heart.

––––––––––

After twelve days of space, without a single word between us, I asked Juan if we could meet. I was ready to officially end it with a break-up letter that I had tucked between the pages of an antique copy of *One Thousand and One Nights*, his favorite. (The fact that I bought him a break-up gift is ridiculous, I know, and demonstrates my desperation to be liked by all, including my exes.)

We sat on a bench facing the fountain in the triangular park, Parque Centenario, and, after a bit of small talk, both said we had something to tell one another.

"You go first," I said. Mistake.

Juan handed me a crumpled invitation for his law school graduation. "I can only invite three people," he said. "I invited my mom, my aunt, and I want you to be there."

Shit, that was sweet. I slyly slipped the break-up letter out from between the pages and said yes. I had vilified text messages for how they enable a quick, thoughtless decision that can change an entire life, but turns out I could make quick, thoughtless decisions in person, too. Next thing I knew, I was right back in the doting girlfriend role, serving hors d'oeuvres at his graduation reception with all his family and friends present.

---

1. Elías did end up giving his support for me writing about him in this book. We are still friends.

BIG BUTT

J uan and I were in Plaza Trinidad like any other night, joking around and drinking boxed red wine out of plastic cups with friends, including his best friends Martín and Omar. Omar had been mocking everyone, as usual, so I decided to give him a taste of his own medicine, with a quip about how he loved the sound of his own voice. But Omar didn't like to be teased, so he fired back.

"I'm Juan," Omar said in his nasally voice, lips puckered. "My girlfriend, she is kind of fat. She needs to go to the gym."

He had pulled the trigger on a sensitive subject. I said nothing but grabbed for Juan's arm to my left and squeezed to indicate it was time to go, now, before I cried.

I remember when I first started believing I was fat. I was six years old, at a slumber party, and a skinny girl pulled my underwear out of my duffel, held them up in front of everyone and said, "You've got a big butt!"

Since then, my whole life had been a constant cycle of self-deprecation and self-doubt, constant fad diets and fasts and fear that my "big butt" made me ugly and unlovable. (This happened far before societal beauty standards had shifted to perceiving a big butt as a positive thing, which just goes to show how silly said standards are—in flux and subjective.)

Juan had heard Omar make the comment, but he said nothing, and that hurt me even more. It brought me back to nearly the same situation that occurred with John years ago, when his best friend called me fat and John stood by, silent.

Juan and I said some quick goodbyes to the group and, as soon as we were beyond the ears and eyes of the group, I broke into tears.

"What's wrong, sweetheart?" Juan asked.

"What's wrong? Omar is an asshole, that's what's wrong."

"Because of that? Because of what he said? Why would you believe that?"

"Because I am." I cried there on the dark street on the way back to the apartment.

"But you're not fat, so why in the world would you think Omar was serious?" He looked puzzled that I had taken the comment seriously.

"I'm sensitive about that, okay? I can't believe you said nothing, that you didn't defend me."

"Erin, you know that we all call Omar 'The Dictator.' He is the clown of the group. No one takes him seriously. He can't take teasing and so sometimes he goes too far and says mean things that aren't true."

By now we had reached the apartment and climbed the four stories in silence. We got to the room, and I stripped off my clothes to get ready for bed.

"Nena, you shouldn't take him seriously," Juan said.

I pushed past him into the bathroom and brushed my

teeth while looking in the mirror at my fat face, made fatter and puffier from tears. Juan stepped into the tiny bathroom and stood behind me. I turned to get out of his way, but he held me there by my waist and spun me around to face myself.

"Look at you," he said.

"No, Juan, I just want to go to bed." I tried to turn and push past him again, but he held firm.

"I think you're crazy. Look at this little waist," he said, squeezing. "You think that with this little waist you are fat?" I whimpered and tried to get out of the small space, away from the menacing mirror. He held me still and poked my ribs with an index finger.

"Look. I can feel your ribs. You are not fat. You actually need to eat. Look." He poked again.

"No, it's...it's my butt," I said, turning to the side and standing on my toes to look at and hate my big butt.

"This butt, nena, that's genetics. It's genetics. And it's beautiful." He squeezed my butt hard and slapped it, and I couldn't help but laugh.

"Okay, okay. I know you like it." I pushed past him and went for the bed, where I laid down and faced the wall, smiling.

Juan came over and crawled into bed behind me, spooning me. I rolled over to face him and kissed him softly, gratefully.

"Eres hermosa," Juan said. *You're beautiful.*

In the moment, I thought he was silly. I thought he was saying what a good boyfriend should say. But, the next day, when I got dressed, I looked in the mirror, and I saw something different. I saw my waist. I saw my ribs. I turned to the side, and I liked my butt.

In Colombia, a big butt is accepted, coveted even. Women go to the plastic surgeon in droves requesting butt implants so they can look as "fat" as I do. A Colombian woman had even said to me a few weeks earlier, in a complimentary tone, "No eres gordita, no eres flaquita, eres LLENI-TA." *You're not fat, you're not skinny, you're FULL.*

I liked that idea. I was full. Full of good food, full of joy, full of worth—regardless of my size and society's lies.

TE UH-OH

I n the Spanish language, there are two ways to say "I love you." *Te quiero* is more like, "I really care about you." It's appropriate for a new relationship or close friends. *Te amo,* on the other hand, is the all-out, stomach-flipping, heart-fluttering, in-love kind of I love you, reserved for only the most serious of feelings. It was an important nuance of the language, one that could change everything.

One night, a wine-drinking night in Getsemaní like any other, Gina, Juan and I went to Mamallena bar. Juan was inside, talking to a friend, and Gina and I stumbled out to the street seeking standing room. We leaned against the building with our two-for-one mojitos in plastic cups and began one of our usual chats about the Colombian dating world and our place among it.

"It's so weird, but I feel like things have changed," I told her. "I was so leery of him. I thought he was such a woman-izer, but now I'm really starting to trust him."

"He has changed so much since he's been with you. I hated him when I first met him, but now I like him for you."

"Everyone likes him. He's always positive and patient, never judgmental. I think, maybe, I love him."

"Aww Er, that's so sweet," Gina said, at the same time that Juan emerged from the bar and joined us out on the street.

"Hey, nena," he said, grabbing my face and giving me a kiss. "Are you okay?" he asked, noticing my watery eyes.

I explained in Spanish what I had told Gina, and he listened, eyes soft and grateful.

"Es por eso que, te amo," I said. *It's for that reason that, I love you.*

He heard me but couldn't believe it. "Qué?" *What?*

"Te amo," I said again.

"¿De verdad?" *Really?* He still didn't believe it. I hugged him and nodded my cheek against his cheek.

"Te amo, también," he told me, squeezing me tight. *I love you, too.* "I wanted to tell you earlier, but I didn't know if you'd get scared, since it has been such a short time. I've loved you since the moment I saw you. I couldn't help it."

In the morning, after we'd had our breakfast of scrambled eggs with veggies and returned to our single twin bed, Juan asked, "Do you really love me?"

"Why do you ask when I've already told you?"

"Te amo is very serious. Tell me, what does it mean to you?"

"It means," I paused, smiling. "It means that you love everything about that person. You can't help it. You see nothing wrong or ugly in them. You see their full potential, everything that they can be, and it's not that you would ever want to change them, never, but you want them to experience the full happiness of having everything they ever wanted, in the world and within themselves, because you love them. You don't just love things about them, but their entire soul, which looks a lot like yours." I had tears in my eyes. I had gone to another place, as I thought of 'te amo' love, and that place was Adam.

"Do you love me like that?" Juan asked.

I stared down at the sheet. I wanted to love Juan like that. I wanted it with all my broken heart.

"I guess, maybe, I spoke too soon. Te quiero," I said, a weak consolation prize for the real thing. "Mucho."

"Te amo," he said.

44

IT'S NOT MEDIA, IT'S ME

My Colombian visa would expire in a month, and I was spending my days sleeping, drinking, languishing.

It's that I can't find a good café, I thought. I need to have good WiFi to write.

It's that I'm always with Juan, I thought. But Juan had been working eleven hours a day for the past two months.

It's all the stuff there is to do here, the partying, I thought. But my girlfriends had finished their teaching contracts and left six weeks ago.

Before I came to Colombia, it was work. I worked too many hours to write.

It was John. He didn't give me enough alone time.

It was the TV. John always had it on, and no one could think with that constant droning in the background.

It was the house. Once we finished it, I would have more time to focus on what really mattered to me.

It was maintaining the house. Cobwebs and paint chips

and rusting and dusting. How can one be expected to keep up with something that's in a constant state of deterioration?

It was media, professional and personal, popping in and distracting me twenty-four hours a day with messages and posts and tweets and emails and likes and favorites.

But I had taken care to eliminate all of that.

I quit that pesky job.

I left distracting John.

I sold the trap of a TV.

I sold the harrying house.

I stopped doing hair and makeup.

I quit that miserable, murderous media and saved myself a ton of time in wishing happy birthdays, giving friends advice, congratulating people on babies and weddings...

I had simplified my life so much that there was nothing left. With nothing to do or distract or deter, I still wasn't writing, and I had to admit the truth, the truth I had been kicking and screaming and refusing to face my entire life: It wasn't media or any of those things. It was me.

I thought that with media removed that I was going to suddenly and magically be the person I always wanted to be, that I would do yoga and meditate and write a book and learn to salsa and have perfect relationships and call my friends on their birthdays. I did most of those things the first couple of months in Colombia, because I was self-fulfilling my prophecies about my own self-improvement. But, with time, I sank right back into the same procrastination patterns, the same neediness and insecurity and laziness.

Going off social media didn't make me better or happier. Going to Peru didn't make me better or happier. Colombia *did* make me better and happier, but only temporarily, for a few fast months of romance and distraction. I sat up in bed, and I got out my laptop to search flights. CTG to MDE. CTG to BOG. CTG to LAX. CTG to MAD. I knew all the airport codes by heart.

My brother's wife had said I could come stay with her in Carlsbad, California (near San Diego), to keep her company while Cory went away for a few months on a military assignment. My finger hovered over CTG to SAN. I loved Cartagena. I could get a job here, teach English. I could get a residence visa. I could fall in love with Juan, maybe tell him "te amo" one day.

But instead, I booked it. Maybe I would be a better person in San Diego.

45

FACEBOOK BEACON

On August 14, 2014, six months and ten days after my dramatic disconnect, I got back on Facebook, now understanding that it was my mindset more than media that ailed me. It was unceremonious, actually. Everything was as I left it, posts of cute kids, cute pets, pretty girls and content couples.

As I lay in bed trolling the news feed, I laughed. I would never post my real status to Facebook:

Sitting in bed sweating my ass off, eating snacks and contemplating a mid-day nap. #LazyAF

No, I would post the fluffy, fanciful stuff that everyone else did:

Morning yoga, walk on the beach and concert under the stars. #LoveMyLife

Facebook, called by some FacadeBook, has been criticized as only showing the sunny side of life. But, just as I learned that without social media I found other methods for both procrastination and affirmation, prior to the advent of social media people also had other methods of putting on airs. Humans are humans, and the need for acceptance and belonging doesn't fundamentally change with the introduction of a new medium.

It's not like, before Facebook, you saw people forthrightly publicizing their marital problems, depression and overall feeling of incompleteness and disappointment with life. No, they put on a smile, and they paraded their "perfect" family in their Sunday best to church or the community fourth of July picnic, so everyone could see that they were happy. People have always controlled their images. We've just changed the size of the stage, exchanged small town events for a global news feed.

So, when I got back on Facebook, it didn't feel like a facade at all, but a beacon of positivity and hope. Here, everyone was putting their best foot forward, the version of themselves they wanted to be, and, filtered or not, it made me smile to see people hugging, smiling and loving, encouraging one another. (And I should note that, in the last several years, people have become much more vulnerably vocal about the struggles they face, as well.)

Sure, the happy posts don't tell the whole story, but we all know that. We all know that she doesn't always look that put-together and that his new car comes with a sixty-hour work week and that their pristine travel photos don't show the parasite-induced diarrhea. But if we love people, we see the best in them, so who are we to judge them for trying to see and show the best of themselves?

Now, having left the social media scene for over six

months, I could see the best in it. I liked Facebook, and I liked all my friends' posts. It was good to be back.

46

ADIÓS, MI VIDA

The night before my flight to San Diego, I lay in bed and sobbed a heart-aching, chest-gurgling sob.

"It's okay. It's going to be okay. It's just a couple of months," Juan tried to comfort me, but I cried harder and he also began to cry. "Why are you crying so hard? We're going to see each other again, right?" We had talked about him getting a U.S. visa so he could come visit around Christmas time, but I knew deep down that it wouldn't happen.

"Yeah," I said. I wasn't crying for Juan, but it was good that he thought so.

I felt disappointed in myself for leaving a life, a very good life, behind. I felt broken, like I couldn't commit to anything and would keep on packing up and moving on for the rest of my life, leaving behind good things in search of great things that possibly didn't exist.

I looked around my apartment that I had cleaned up and made cozy with its bright-colored sheets and turquoise bath-mat. I thought of Beni and Dolores, who said their *casa* was *mi casa*. I thought of friends I was just getting to know, like

Yeri, who, as we walked together one day, said in her broken English, "I want stay here."

"You want to stay here in Cartagena?" I asked her, to clarify.

"No, you. You stay here."

I thought of the labyrinth of cobblestone streets that I had finally managed to navigate with confidence. I had a good life here, and yet, I left. That's why I sobbed, as Juan petted my hair and soaked it with his own loving tears.

The next day, Juan escorted me to the airport.

"Two of you traveling today?" the airline agent asked.

"Just one," Juan answered.

"You better go straight to security," she said. "Your plane's going to board soon."

I looked at him. "I thought we had more time."

I filed through security, and Juan followed along outside the rope corral, looking in like Tiny Tim watching the neighbors carve a fat turkey. It wasn't fair that Colombians weren't allowed to freely travel, that they had to get visas for the U.S. and other destinations. When I got to the door, I looked back at him, at his sad smile.

"Can I say one more goodbye?" I asked the agent lady checking passports and boarding passes.

"Yeah, go ahead," she said, smiling. I walked over to him and gave him a quick kiss.

"Adíos, mi vida," he said, a Colombian term of endearment that seemed more appropriate now than ever. *Goodbye, my life.*

47

ENOUGH

On the red-eye flight to San Diego, I was the only one awake, and I missed him. I missed him so much that the inside of my heart felt like it had been scraped out with a cheese grater and my throat had a wet, clogged feeling. I missed his eyes, the way he saw me and I saw him. I missed his hands, the way he used them when he talked, molding a beautiful piece of art. I missed his words, how he explained everything in a way that made sense to me. I missed his ears, the way they always understood what I was trying to say. I missed his wide grinning mouth, that silly smirk he always made when he was right. I missed Adam.

Though I'd stopped going to the library, the words of my favorite book were still written on my heart. I had wanted so badly for the book to be mine, to have it in my arms, in my bed, where I could open it whenever I wanted to read the secrets it held and caress its torn but lovely pages. I wanted it so much that I neglected to understand one very important thing, something that I only understood now after time away: It didn't have to be mine for me to love it. Adam didn't have to be my lover, because, what I really missed, was my friend.

I got out my laptop to craft the message I would send to him after so many months gone.

August 27, 2014
Dear Adam,

I'll be in town for a few days. Want to have a beer and catch up? I want to tell you all of it.

I miss my friend.

Erin

P.S. See how I broke that up for impact? ;)

I thought about the simple words the rest of the flight home, rewriting them fifty different ways, expounding on them, belaboring them, impregnating them and deleting them. I thought about sending a letter, something far more exciting and dramatic. But I didn't need it to be dramatic. I needed it to be received.

In the end, I emailed precisely what I had started with, as soon as I set my things down in my brother's spare room in Carlsbad. Adam wrote back immediately.

August 27, 2014
Erin!!! I miss you so much! I would love to. I want to hear everything. I am so happy you contacted me. I can't wait to see you. :)

You made my summer. :)

I love the break-up-for-impact technique. It was very
effective. :)

Damn, I miss this.

We were right back to it, ping-ponging back and forth
with lengthy messages as though I hadn't spent the better
part of a year hiding in South America trying to forget him.
I wrote:

I never got one letter from you. I sent you six, and I
wrote more but ultimately gave up. The last one I wrote
was 42 pages and spanned several months of activity,
but it got stolen along with the rest of my stuff on an
island.

And he wrote:

Are you serious that you never recieved any of my
letters? Not one? I sent you HUNDREDS of pages. I
kept daily journals. I wrote something for you EVERY
DAY. If it's true, I may vomit. :(

I am so incredibly sad. I wanted so bad for you to
know that someone was thinking of you every single
day. I started writing before you even left. Damn. I
could cry.

I didn't know what to think. I thought maybe you were
just busy, or maybe you thought what I was writing was

dumb, or maybe you just wanted me to stop writing. I
just didn't know.

I still carry a notebook in my pocket (it's there right now)
with stuff I write down for you. It's partly filled, but I
stopped when it looked like maybe you wouldn't want it.
So, in a weird way I'm super happy that the reason I
didn't hear from you was cuz you didn't hear from me.

Mother fucking postal service.

At first, I was mad at the postal service, too. I knew, from
talking to other friends and family members, that many
people had sent letters that never arrived and that mine
never reached them, either. (Only a few postcards made it.) I
lamented all the lost words that might have comforted me,
showed me Adam still cared. But then I realized that I wasn't
meant to get those letters. Had I received them, even one, my
soul would have stayed back in Oregon with him. It wouldn't
have traveled with me, as such a fine friend. My experience
would have been more performative, attempting to impress
him rather than what it was: pure, unwitnessed joy in spec-
tacular present moments. (And yes, I know Adam spelled
"received" wrong. Maybe it's sort of a nerd's revenge that I
didn't fix it for him before the world.)

I closed my laptop, smiling. The old me would have
carried on chatting for hours, until my fingers ached and my
eyes felt strained, until Adam fell asleep and I tortured
myself wondering if I said something wrong or if he didn't
like me anymore. But not anymore. This was good. This was
enough.

I had hoped quitting media would help me detach from Adam, but it did more than that. It helped me detach from seeking outside approval, from him or anyone else. In only seven months, I had managed to re-program myself. I now checked in with me first, my own heart, to see what I should do and who I should be. I trusted my own feelings—my intuition—and I knew what I had to do next.

As noted earlier, Juan translates to John in English, and I wondered at God's sense of humor. Many Eastern philosophies teach that the universe will keep handing you the same lesson until you learn it. It took me a while—twelve years, eight months and twenty-seven days, to be exact—but a lesson learned, though slowly and reluctantly, is better than no lesson at all. I had to say goodbye, or Juan would be another John.

I couldn't explain it logically, but something had felt amiss since the beginning. He was fun, handsome, adventurous and smart. He loved me, it was clear. But the heart has its reasons, and even if I didn't understand it now, I had to trust myself.

I broke up with Juan over video chat, which he accepted easily, with minimal emotion. Two years later, I would learn from a mutual Colombian friend that Juan had cheated on me during our relationship, with a Mandarin professor at the university. I would also venture to guess he went right back to sleeping around as soon as I left Colombian soil, which is why the break-up didn't affect him much.

As good 'ol Captain Carl said, "Always trust your first

instinct. That's the best one." (True, Carl's instincts led us straight into a reef and a palm tree, but I do believe he had a point.)

48

FLIP PHONING THE TABLES

I had decided I would continue using my basic flip phone in San Diego, which got me all kinds of interesting looks among a population that worships material things.

"Ew, I thought you were poor," said the barista with impeccable beard hair who served me my daily latte.

The flip phone also had the happy, unintended consequence of putting the ball in my court when it came to dating. Men would message me and, considering the effort it takes to text back on a flip phone, I would wait hours or even days before responding.

RANDOM DUDE-BRO I MET

Hey beautiful, sup?

Aren't you even going to respond?

WTF I thought you liked me.

Fine, whatever, forget you.

Hey, you there?

Where, once upon a time, I was that person anxiously watching my phone for responses, I had become the carefree, confident dater while these dudes were spinning out and self-eliminating before I could even respond to their first message.

During this time, I also tried my first-ever foray into online dating, and there, too, I could feel that a big shift had happened. When I went on dates, no matter how cool or handsome the suitors, I never obsessed over what they thought about me. I only thought of whether I liked them, whether they met my standards and expectations for someone who is intelligent, kind, fun and attractive. I slept with no one, because I didn't feel like it. I no longer felt obliged to perform or earn approval.

The other surprise benefit of self-approving over people-pleasing was a massive reduction in the anxiety I had lived with and thought normal my entire life. As I spent less time inside other people's heads, imagining what they wanted from me, I became more present and aware of all the beautiful things life had to offer me.

49

MEDITATION TRANSFORMATION

I started reading *Eat Pray Love*, Elizabeth Gilbert's travel memoir that graced the *New York Times* best seller list for 187 weeks.

While I could certainly relate to her experiences in marriage and travel, I was more intrigued by her description of meditation and *kundalini shakti* in India:

> "In mystical India, as in many shamanistic traditions, *kundalini shakti* is considered a dangerous force to play around with if you are unsupervised; the inexperienced Yogi could quite literally blow his mind with it."

Having no idea what I was getting myself into, I decided to try it. I liked my meditation experience on the sailboat in Colombia, and I wanted to blow my mind. Besides, it wasn't *really* going to work like she said, energy being unleashed up my spine toward God. This was like when my friend Bri and I tried the Ouija board in her attic at age ten. A game.

I lit incense and a candle on the desk. I sat cross-legged

on the floor, next to my air mattress in my brother's spare room, and I began to focus on my breath.

To my surprise, this time, for the first time in my life, there was no mental chatter. I was transported immediately to a space of stillness. My physical body dissolved, and I felt a part of the space around me. I felt an intense tingling, in my limbs, in my spine.

I freaked out. The kundalini was going to get me and explode my head! I opened my eyes, blew out the candle, and did what I always do when I'm scared. I Googled.

meditation

I was in too deep. I needed someone to tell me how to do this right. The first Google result was a free meditation group taking place that Sunday in Encinitas, ten miles from me. I RSVP'ed, felt relief and went to sleep.

That night, I had a terrifying dream.

My brother's wife and I were in an old house, and the windows and doors were all open, because Bri was coming soon and we wanted to surprise her. We looked outside and saw a blue Cadillac sitting in the driveway with a man inside who had an ominous, chilling presence.

Bri walked up to the house on one side while the man approached on the other, headed toward the open door. We couldn't simply shut the door to the bad man, because we would shut Bri out, too.

The man entered first, and I could feel that he intended to do us harm. I had a gun and tried to shoot him but dropped it on the floor. I scrambled for it and pointed it up at him from my place on the floor, but when I fired, it had no bullets. He laughed in my face.

I woke up. As my heart pounded, rain pounded the roof, and palm leaves blew horizontally outside my window. A storm within, a storm without. I prayed, afraid.

Elizabeth Gilbert also described nightmares after her kundalini experience, so I wondered if my mind was simply fulfilling the expectations I held upon reading her story, both of the meditation sensation and the subsequent nightmare. I had ingested a prose placebo.

Either way, mind or higher power, the experience was perspective-altering, as I recognized the power of our minds to create an experience which, for the experiencer, is very real. If a higher power created that feeling of oneness and connectedness, then It existed—God or the Sage or Yahweh or any of the thousands of names that try to capture that greatness.

If my mind created the feeling, that also meant that an intangible power, the power of thought, was able to produce a palpable experience. I should have known this from daily experience. I could think the intangible thought, "Adam doesn't love me," and a tangible experience of pain in my chest would ensue.

Dreams are always symbolic, and I had an idea what mine symbolized. I had opened the doors to the house of my mind, and I didn't have the tools to defend myself against the bad that may enter with the good. Guided meditation was the beginning to acquiring those tools.

"Focus on the breath. Breathing in, breathing out. Belly rising, belly falling." Larry the meditation guru had the most calming voice, and it didn't feel scary with his guidance.

He and his lovely Brazilian wife Miriam opened their home to strangers once a week, asking nothing, to teach the transcendental, peaceful art of meditation. He had left corporate life in his early twenties and traveled throughout Asia, where he learned about meditation and became a teacher himself, having taught for more than twenty years now.

I was so nervous, and I felt stupid for feeling nervous. This isn't a big deal. What's wrong with you? Why do you have to be so nervous and anxious all the time? I would soon learn that nearly everyone who comes to meditation for the first time feels nervous. I was not alone.

I'd had a persistent cough for the past week, and I was worried that I wouldn't be able to control it, that it would interrupt the other meditators and I'd get kicked out of meditation class. But seconds into the forty-five-minute mediation, Larry provided the answer to my fear, as though he were speaking directly to my busy mind.

"If you feel any discomfort in the body, focus your attention on it. Feel it intimately. Do not resist it."

I focused on the tickle in my throat. Where previously my thoughts were, "Don't cough don't cough don't cough you idiot," I listened to Larry and I felt the tickle, observing it, not judging, not resisting, not fearing.

"Sometimes, our bodies just want some attention. Like a baby crying for its mother. Hold it. Give it your attention, and the discomfort will dissolve." I didn't cough for the entire session, and the cough was completely gone thereafter.

Larry also taught the technique of naming, which was much like what I had learned from *The I Ching* when I was on the sailboat.

"Watch each thought come and go, not judging. Give it a name, but don't resist. Anger, if the feeling is anger. Planning, if it is a plan. Watch them come and go. It's okay to feel whatever you feel."

He then talked us through a body scan.

"Feel each sensation of the body. Feel the sitting bones. Feel the right big toe, the middle toe, the third toe, the fourth toe, the pinky toe..."

When Larry rang the ending bell, I couldn't believe it. Forty-five minutes felt like five. I felt relaxed but energized. I realized that the reason I felt so tired all the time, why I sometimes slept twelve hours a day, was because of the incessant chatter in my head, stressing, criticizing, arguing.

I became a meditation addict. I went to see Larry every Sunday, and I meditated every night by myself before bed. My head was becoming quieter with every day, and my life prospered as a result. Without Worry and Fear in the way, other things like Creativity, Inspiration and Gratitude were able to get in the door.

50

THE PRESENCE PILL

J ust as fate and the ever-expanding universe bring us to the right people at the right time, they also bring us the right lessons. "When the student is ready, the teacher will appear," says a Buddhist proverb.

Before I left Oregon, *The Power of Now,* by Eckhart Tolle, was recommended to me by Chloe, the "I don't believe in God" girl who got this whole belief ball rolling two years ago.

I'd forgotten about the recommendation, until I sat at a bar with my friend Andrew, a therapist whom I'd met on my recreational volleyball team. (We had bonded over the fact that we both sucked.) I whined to him about one of the things I always whined about, a lost love, a lonely feeling, a lack of direction.

"I can understand that," he said, nodding. He looked like a stretched-out Hank Azaria who wore socks with sandals. "But do you have any problem right now?"

"Well yeah, just what I said. My ex-boyfriend Juan hates

me. And I hate that he thinks everything we shared was false, that I didn't care."

"Right now. On this razor's edge of time. Sitting at this bar, talking to me, drinking a cold beer. Your ex isn't here right now." He tried. I stared dumbly at him.

"Have you read *The Power of Now*? I'm re-reading it again now. I read it at least once a year."

"I've heard of it before. Another friend I really respect recommended it. Guess it's time to give it a shot."

The Power of Now for me was like taking a presence pill. Its teachings made me instantly aware of how much mental energy I spent in the unchangeable past or unknowable future.

Everything became more vibrant. For the first time in my life fully present, it was as though a cloudy veil had been lifted from my eyes. I began to see things for the first time. Trees had curves and definition I'd never noticed. Sunsets were so brilliant I felt I was a part of them, that I could reach out and dip my hand in the stretched-taffy skies. I felt joy that made me cry and skip and dance. I befriended strangers. I ran until my legs burned. And I wrote like never before, no longer fearing future judgments or lamenting wasted time. I enjoyed every keystroke, every page, every moment.

51

INTO THE DESERT

Every day, I went to The Chocolate Bar café in Carlsbad (sounds rough, I know). I wrote for eight to ten ecstatic hours, until they were stacking chairs and shutting off lights.

One day, engrossed in my writing as ever, a petite Mexican girl with waist-length, shiny hair interrupted me and motioned to her laptop on the table behind me.

"Excuse me. Would you watch my things while I pee?"

"Of course. If you'll watch my things while I pee."

Established pee partners, we began to chat (after peeing, of course).

"Thank you. I'm Evelyn. I just moved here from Chicago, so I don't know anyone."

"I'm Erin. I just moved here, too. What do you do?"

"I'm a writer," she said, with confidence.

"Me too! What do you write?"

"I've written a book. Have you ever read *The Alchemist*?"

"It's my new favorite book," I said, having just read Paulo Coelho's world-renowned classic.

She touched her hand to her chest and laughed. "It's my favorite, too. I've read it so many times. My book is kind of like that, about following your heart."

"I have to read it."

She wrote down the title of the book, *La Fuerza de Tu Esencia*, and her details. Evelyn would become one of my best friends, a constant loving presence to remind me that fate does take us to the right places and people. If ever I worried about anything, she would say in her beautiful Mexican accent, "Amiga, don't worry about it." And I listened.

Everything worked out when we were together, as if fueled by our combined belief.

Missed the last train from San Diego to Carlsbad?

"Don't worry about it," Evelyn would say, and someone trustworthy would offer us a ride home.

No reservation at the wine bar?

"Don't worry about it." They would have a cancellation right as we walked in.

Coming down with a cold?

"Don't worry about it...and drink some tequila." The cold would clear right up.

In *The Alchemist*, the protagonist Santiago finds his soul mate, named Fátima, in an oasis in the desert. San Diego was my oasis and Evelyn was my Fátima, which we affectionately called one another throughout our many adventures. But, just as Santiago left the oasis to pursue his "Personal Legend" in the desert beyond, I felt compelled to do the same. My heart pulled me relentlessly toward something more. But was my heart worth trusting?

My heart had believed Adam was my soul mate. The pull that I felt toward him could not be explained as anything other than divine, ordained by the cosmos that our two distinct lives should intertwine. Everything inside me knew that he and I were meant to meet, just as he had said that drunken night at the office.

So, when he didn't want me, when he wasn't in love with me, I had to resign and accept that my heart was wrong. That was the worst pain of all, worse than the heartbreak, worse than the loneliness, was admitting that I could not trust in my intuition.

But now, I understood that *my heart was right.* My heart led me to Adam, because Adam led me to my heart. Our relationship brought me back to writing again—something that gave me chills throughout my entire body greater than any physical touch could ever elicit, that brought tears of joy and laughter.

I recalled the Peruvian shaman, his words to me almost exactly one year earlier: "If you can work not just with your head, but with your heart, you will be very rich."

So, now trusting in my heart completely, I listened. I booked a one-way ticket to London leaving in three months —scheduled to arrive on my thirtieth birthday—with no real plan but to follow my heart, no matter what.

THE WHOLE NARANJA

Adam and I continued to be friends, only friends, messaging one another every day, offering support and reporting on how many words we had written toward our respective manuscripts. But I no longer asked him to edit my work. Too risky.

While he did encourage me to express aspects of myself that I couldn't with my ex-husband, I realized that I clambered after Adam's approval also, in different ways. For his approval, I read books I found uninteresting, drank whisky I didn't drink, smoked cigars I didn't smoke. My propensity to please would be something I would always need to watch with awareness, whenever I felt myself slipping away from my soul and into a persona curated for someone else.

When Adam came into my life with all his attention and words of affirmation, I felt like I was finally whole. I thought this meant he was my other orange half, my *media naranja* who could complete me, know me better than myself and all those other romantic clichés.

Conversely, I thought that, without him, I should feel

incomplete, a disgusting miserable mess, oozing into a pathetic puddle until my other half could come and sweep me up into a person again.

But now I knew. Adam wasn't my media naranja nor was Juan or anyone else, for that matter. I was the whole naranja —the whole fucking orange—all on my own. Each time I said out loud what I really wanted or believed, I was whole. Each time I wrote for me and no one else, I was whole. Each time I acted authentically instead of performatively, I was whole. Each time I meditated or otherwise managed to be fully present, I was whole. And I was done giving up segments of myself, for anyone.

In knowing my wholeness and Adam's purpose in my life, eight days before my flight to London, I was finally ready to let him go.

On January 6, 2015 (via Facebook Messenger)
Dear Adam,

I love you, and I loved you more than anyone I had ever loved. Until today.

Today, I love myself more.

Today, I am joyful.
Today, I am peaceful.
Today, I am strong.
Today, I am whole.
And for those reasons, today, I say,

Goodbye.

I love you, and a piece of me always will, but in my journey I have learned that I don't need you.

Not to teach me.
Not to inspire me.
Not to value me.
Not to encourage me.
Not to understand me.
Not to make me laugh.
Not to love me.

I also don't need you to respond to this, and, actually, I ask that you don't. I know that you understand. You always do.

So, this is a love letter, to myself, saying goodbye to you, forever, because my heart deserves to be free. I can't carry you in my heart anymore.

I wish you so much joy. So much peace. So much love.

I wish you all the things I feel in me today, and more.

With love and gratitude,
Erin

Adam responded with only a single, blue thumbs-up symbol. Considering that he had insisted, a few weeks earlier, that our continuous conversation must never end, I interpreted his blue thumbs-up as containing some pain, some passive aggression, some "fine-if-that's-what-you-really-want." Or maybe it didn't. Maybe he was ready to remove the complication of me, also, so he could focus on his marriage.

Whatever the case, I knew I had come a long way, because I didn't agonize over what *he* thought, *he* felt, *he* meant—all of which were unknowable. I knew I had done the right thing for *my* heart, and I rested in that knowing.

EPILOGUE

I sat by my departure gate at LAX airport, scheduled to leave just before sunset. I would turn thirty somewhere over the Atlantic in the middle of the night and would arrive at Gatwick in London the following afternoon. My friend Brian, whom I had met volunteering at the Peruvian orphanage last year, would pick me up and take me back to his shared flat in Finsbury Park, where an air mattress awaited me.

My excitement always gets me to the airport way too early, but I wasn't the only one. A handsome man with a five o'clock shadow, slouchy beanie and big brown eyes sat across from me and smiled. Here we go. Yes, I was the whole naranja, but my heart was wide open and ready to be followed! His name was Joshua, but he went by "Shua," perhaps trying to sound cool and unique seeing as he was an aspiring actor. But he didn't seem to have an ounce of ego in him, and he was funny and just as excited as I was for this first-time European adventure. Also in his early thirties, he also had a one-way ticket to London and also planned to stay with a friend.

When we boarded, we begged a middle-aged man to switch seats so we could sit next to one another, and then we talked excitedly and loudly the entire flight, with several people shushing us as the hour approached Midnight. At 11:59, he bought me a birthday beer and we toasted to my thirtieth, already shaping up to be the best of my life. We giggled like little children, and the shushing of other passengers just made us laugh harder.

"You know what I really want?" he asked.

"What?"

"A jump suit!"

"Me too! The whole reason I studied journalism was because of April O'Neil with the yellow jump suit."

"From Ninja Turtles!"

"YES!"

"Let's get jump suits and run all around London together," he said.

"YES!"

"Shhhhhhh," came the aggressive shushing. I have no idea why the other passengers weren't intensely interested in our intellectual musings.

Once we landed, we practically frolicked together through the required proceedings until we arrived at the row of customs agents lined up before us like grocery store checkout counters. We each were directed to a different agent, the final step before setting foot on British ground. Shua passed through with ease (despite the fact that he was planning to work illegally there), but my agent had a resentful face and a bone to pick with me.

"You're a *writer*?" He said it like a dirty word, looking down at my self-proclaimed profession on the customs form.

"Yes!" I said in a chipper tone.

"And you're staying with a *friend*?" he asked, looking at Brian's name and address on the form.

"Yes!"

"You sure he's not your *boyfriend*?" Again, with the dirty-word inflection.

"I'm sure. He's just a friend."

"Yeah, right," the agent said, all but growling at me. This was when I first caught on that I might actually be in trouble here.

"Why do you just have a one-way ticket?" Aggro Agent asked.

"Because I'm going to travel through Europe over land."

"Where are you going next?"

Shit, I didn't know. Don't people do this, backpack through Europe and make up their minds as they go along?

"Paris," I lied. "I'm going to take the underground Chunnel to Paris in a couple weeks."

"This isn't looking good for you," he said, as he glared into my lying soul and scribbled a handwritten note in my passport, something I had never seen in all my border entries past. Can he do that? I looked beyond the desk to where Shua stood waiting on the other side, craning his neck to see what was happening with his beautiful browns full of hope and concern.

I was ready to follow my heart, to frolic gleefully through iconic London in a sweet jump suit with my new bestie, but I somehow hadn't considered that the heart doesn't always get what it wants. Shouldn't I know that already, from the last two years of unrequited love? Hadn't I learned anything? The heart throws its tantrums like a toddler child, screaming "I want it" on repeat without rationale or recourse, and the universe steps in like the loving parent to say, "It's not for you, my love. Have this instead."

SNEAK PEEK OF THE SEQUEL

Visit **onloveandtravel.com** to sign up for a notification when the sequel is released!

In Chefchaouen, Morocco, a city best known for being almost entirely painted blue, I experienced two important aspects of Moroccan culture: one titillating and the other humiliating.

As I climbed the surrounding hills, I paused to look down on a place that looks more like a Van Gogh painting than reality. At that moment, a beautiful song began to echo out from the mosques and reverberate through the city, up into the hills where I stood, awed.

A man's soulful voice, clear and imbued with reverent passion, sang the same pattern over and over again. As one somehow intuitively understands the meaning behind an Italian opera, without speaking Italian, I understood the meaning of this song in my soul before the words were explained to me. "God is great. Come to worship. God is great. Come to worship."

Where I thought I had little in common with Morocco's culture or its people, I felt connectedness now. The yearning in the singing man's voice sounded like my own, as I laid in bed some nights, yearning for guidance, for love. Our differences were just distractions covering up that one universal desire.

Now feeling more Moroccan, I decided to go to an authentic Moroccan hammam. A hammam is a public bath house, a literal watering hole where women (or men, depending on the hour) gather to wash and gossip.

It took me a while to find the place, and I felt a sense of urgency as I wandered alone through the labyrinthine medina, the old city. Though I had felt connectedness, I had also felt my bum grabbed last week in Tangier, so I didn't desire to be alone for any more time than necessary. I asked people for the hammam at every turn, and, finally, I arrived at an unimpressive, unmarked building with a ten-foot-high stack of wood out front.

I timidly pushed in the swinging door to find what looked like a 1970s YMCA locker room, with a check-in counter to my left and naked women drying themselves in front of me. I approached the middle-aged woman at the desk.

"English?"

She shook her head no. I mimed washing myself, and she sold me a scrubber mitt and the scentless Berber soap, which looks like a blob of melty brown sugar, served in a twisted plastic bag.

I mimed massaging myself, since I'd been advised to purchase the massage package, and she pointed to another woman whom I would best describe as sturdy, walking around in only wet, white granny panties. I understood that this would be my masseuse. It's incredible the "conversations" you can achieve through mime.

The only non-Moroccan there, I kept to my corner and slowly undressed, stealing glances at the other women to assure I was undressing the right way and to the right degree. They all wore plain, cotton underwear, but I had on a swimsuit, which made me feel self-conscious. It looked too flashy. I took off the top to blend in a little better.

I slipped on the rubber sandals they provided and followed the other women through a door, past a warm, mid-sized room into a warmer, larger one beyond.

Here, in the large, tiled steam room, more than thirty women sat bathing themselves and one another. I stood up against a wall, thinking that if I looked as uncomfortable as I felt, one of the women would surely see that I'm foreign and show me how this all works. But no one approached.

Sturdy Gurdy came buffaloing into the room and looked at me with a stern protruding forehead. She pointed to the ground and I obeyed, sitting like a compliant pet, and then she left.

Maybe it's my American paranoia, but this "bath" did not feel sanitary. A woman to my left was dumping a bucket of water into her underwear, the results of which would come sloshing out and flowing in my direction.

The back wall boasted a tile throne of sorts, with steps up to three sinks where the women could fill their buckets. The women sitting on these steps appeared to be the Queen Bees. They leaned back against the steps as other women scrubbed them furiously and shared the week's news.

Many of the women were in good form, which you wouldn't know from the loose-fitting, floor-grazing djellabas that they wear in public. Seeing their curvy, fit bodies, it was hard not to imagine what they'd look like in Western garb, a pair of cut-off jean shorts and a crop top. They'd look smokin' hot. But they didn't care about looking smokin' hot, and it put our Western priorities in bleak perspective.

I am ashamed to admit that a large portion of my mental energy throughout my life has been consumed by trying to look smokin' hot. Endless diets, workouts, waxing, shopping, moisturizing, painting, dyeing, weighing, crying. And why do we do it? So we can attract the opposite sex and be the envy of the same sex. There was none of that here. The women seemed to have body blinders on, and though they came in all shapes and sizes, there appeared to be no distinction of "better" or "worse." They just were. Skinny was as good as curvy. Big-breasted as good as small. Wrinkled as good as taut. White as good as brown.

They washed one another intimately, reaching every place, without any indication of sexuality considered. They washed one another's breasts, armpits, backs, hair. The women would wash their own private parts, reaching into their underpants, without any shyness or shame.

After about twenty minutes seated on the floor watching this, I wondered where Sturdy Gurdy was and decided maybe there was a miscommunication and I should go find her. I found her in the locker room, where she frowned and flailed her arms like an air traffic controller, waving me back toward the steam room. I tucked my tail between my legs and sheepishly returned to my spot on the floor to wait another thirty minutes.

By this time I really had enough and sneaked back to the locker room where I began to get dressed. The ten dollars I paid would have to be a wash, or rather, a no-wash. But Gurdy caught me. Her brow protruded even more intensely and her arms flailed even more wildly. I would have thought she'd want to pocket the money without the work, but she insisted, through mime, that I go back and sit the fuck down (I imagine she was saying).

This time she did enter behind me, and she signaled for me to lie on my stomach on the wet, warm tile floor. Now the genitalia juices were sloshing toward my face.

She grabbed my scrubber, squatted beside me with thighs like a sumo wrestler, and began to scrub my body with such violent motion that I clung to the tiles by my fingernails. I had imagined a relaxing day spa experience, and this felt more like a CIA torture scene.

She mimed for me to flip over and proceeded to torture my front half, her large saggy breasts nearly hitting me in the face with every scrub upward. She accosted my armpits and held up the scrubber to show me the gray accumulation of dead skin as if to say, "You nasty, girl."

After scrubbing almost every square centimeter of my body, she got up and I sat up, dazed and abused. I wondered about the "massage" portion but didn't dare ask. As I started to regain consciousness, looking around the room and feeling like a survivor, she dumped a cold bucket of water over my head.

"Aghhh!" I sputtered from the shock of the cold in the warm room. She put her hands on her hips and looked at me as if to say, "Are we done here?" I nodded frantically, and Sturdy Gurdy moved on to her next victim.

IN APPRECIATION

Spoiler Alert:
*Skip the final paragraph if you want to
avoid seeing a hint at where life takes me after the sequel.*

I think most writers would tell you that the most valuable thing people contributed to their publishing journey is simply belief, the knowledge that we can do this hard thing even when we don't believe it ourselves. There are some people in my life who continually reminded me I could do it, over nine years of my tortured-artist whining, and they are, truly, the only reason this book exists in the world today. I don't know why we writers are like this, but, alas, we are inalterably dramatic, and I am inalterably thankful to the friends and family who propped up my delicate ego along the way.

To Alexa Trost, my dear friend. We met because you tucked my tag into my dress at salsa night. We locked eyes, and I knew we would be friends forever. You were one of my first readers, and you made me know it has its audience. You listened to me try about one thousand titles, and you told everyone I would be famous. You have conquered more hard things than I ever have, and you make it look easy while being always kind, graceful, beautiful.

To Clay Coppedge, my inspirational author uncle. You are the person I point to and say, "Look, he does it! He writes for a living, and he is killing it!" I love you and I'm so thankful for the feedback you gave as one of my first readers. You told me I should split it into two books, and I doubted. I realized five years later you were right. You have always offered sound advice without judgment, always with support.

To Kirsten Fountain, my former teacher, now friend. Who would have known, when you taught me social studies at thirteen years old, that one day we would be supporting each other on publishing journeys? Your belief in me and in something bigger than all of us gives me strength. Your love gives me a space in which I can be my most authentic self. I love you, and you are love.

To Randy Pollard, my dad, and Trish Pollard, my stepmom. You have read every article I ever shared. You helped me pay for the writers conference where I could pitch my stories. It wasn't so much the money but that investment in me, that belief, that knowing that I was going to take it and make something of it. You never judged any of my batshit-crazy life decisions and, to the contrary, championed going after whatever weird thing I ever felt a calling to chase. I love you.

To Beverly Brooks, my mama, and Bob Baldwin, my stepdad. You, mama, were the first one who instilled me with the belief that I could do anything, that I was going to take on the world and that I was going to win. You sought out the best teachers at every school, the best experiences, the best of everything so I could be strong and smart and confident. I love you, and I know that everything I will ever accomplish is because you loved me so deeply. Bob, thank you for the support you have given us for many years, for the strong support you are for my mama.

To Tyler Johnson and Mya Zelinka. Tyler, you have given your ears, your time, your words of encouragement and your full support to me and this project. Thank you for designing a gorgeous cover and for being the most amazing, loving dad to Mya. Mya, you are our baby girl, the reason it's important to share stories of boldly being who we really are. You are one thousand percent yourself, knowing what you want and letting us know it loudly from the day you were born, and I am so thankful for you. I love you, and I love the strong woman you are becoming.